Bitter Fruit

Bitter Fruit

The Betrayal of the Enlightenment

John Smythies

Center for Brain and Cognition
University of California San Diego

and

Institute of Neurology
University of London

ISBN : 1-4196-4279-0

Library of Congress Control Number: 2006907224

To order additional copies, please contact us.
BookSurge, LLC
www.booksurge.com
1-866-308-6235
orders@booksurge.com

Bitter Fruit

vii

Contents

Waste not your Hour, nor in the vain pursuit
of This or That endeavour and dispute.
Better be merry with the fruitful Grape
Than sadden after none, or bitter, Fruit.

Omar Khayyám

Acknowledgements

This book has benefited from discussions over the years with numerous people. These include A.J. Ayer, John Beloff, Lord Brain, C.D. Broad, Bernard Carr, Francis Crick, Richard Dawkins, Robert Eisner, Rosalind Heywood, Aldous Huxley, Carl Gustav Jung, Heinrich Klüver, Arthur Koestler, Andrei Linde, Edward Osborn, H.H. Price, Ian Stevenson, Avrum Stroll, Sir Francis Walshe, and Edmund Wright. I am also grateful for their continued support to Michael Trimble and Vilayanur Ramachandran, to Lenora Cornelius for her invaluable editorial assistance, and to Nick Rezmerski for invaluable help with the art cover for this book

INTRODUCTION

Part 1.

The 20th Century was the most violent in human history marred by two World Wars, the Holocaust, Hiroshima, and the great Stalinist Terror. The XXIst Century promises to be worse. No sooner had the threat posed to Western civilization by the secular religions of National Socialism and Soviet Communism been beaten back by the heirs of the Enlightenment, than a new and deadly threat has appeared on the horizon. This is the triangular conflict between a virulent form of Islamic extremism, a revived Christian fundamentalism, and the nihilistic doctrines of reductionist materialism that threatens to take place on a stage illuminated by the relentless spread of terrorism and nuclear blackmail. These ideological tectonic plates threaten to collide with disastrous results for us all. The heirs to the Enlightenment have never been in so great a danger.

Some time ago the distinguished ethologist Richard Dawkins expressed the opinion that religion poses the greatest danger to world peace in this uncertain world. This prophecy was greeted mainly by skepticism and derision. However, the tenor of recent events suggests that he may well be right—although not exactly in the way he proposed. During the Age of Reason, people came, largely under the influence of Descartes, Newton, Locke, Diderot, Jefferson, Franklin and Hume, to believe that human problems could be solved by the application of practical reason—in other words by an enlightened philosophy and science. In this existence, it was believed, that people lived in a world whose harmony and grace were underwritten by Newton's *Principia*. Their psychological confidence was guaranteed by the Christian religion whose intellectual underpinning was provided by the dualistic Cartesian theory of mind. This theory taught that humans are composed of a mortal physical body and an immortal spirit that, after the death of the physical body, enters into another realm of existence within the confines of the teaching of the Church. In the Moslem world, Newton and the philosophers of the Enlightenment played no role. Instead faith in this world and belief in one's entry into the next were both guaranteed by one source — the Word of God as revealed in the Koran. In India the Hindu religion, and its offshoot Buddhism, were based on a more ancient wisdom expressed in the Upanishads and the Vedanta. These religions also supported a dualist theory of mind that allowed for the existence of an immortal soul.

In the West, the last half of the 19ᵗʰ century witnessed the almost total collapse of this system, that had previously supported Western Civilization, at the hands of a new generation of scientists and philosophers, of whom the most prominent were Darwin, Marx, Freud and Nietzsche. The first and leading blow was struck by Charles Darwin who demonstrated that many of the key teachings of the Christian Church were entirely erroneous. Men and women were not specially created but were merely rather intelligent and successful animals that had evolved, like all other animals, from lower organisms, according to the principles of random genetic mutation and natural selection. At the same time, early brain scientists were expressing the opinion that their investigations had shown that humans did not have souls either and that a human being consisted merely of a physical body. No part of a person, in fact and not fancy, survived the disintegration of the physical body at death. A human mind was identical *in toto* with the activity of various neurons in the brain. So the human soul vanished, along with phlogiston and unicorns, from serious scientific consideration. This change in man's outlook on his world did not of course occur overnight. The battle raged for the next century but it is true to say that this account is believed by nearly all contemporary scientists and philosophers. This revolution has had serious social consequences as we will see.

The next axe was swung by Karl Marx. Darwin's new theory naturally raised a problem. If the Christian religion, and indeed most religions, are as wrong as Darwin claimed, why had they lasted so long and had exerted such a grip on human loyalty and imagination? Marx provided one rational answer. Religion was, he claimed, the opium of the people used by the have's (the Capitalist class, and earlier by the Feudal barons) to clamp the have-not's (the peasants and workers) more firmly in their chains. By dangling false promises of a glorious life to come (especially one in which poor men enter Heaven more easily than rich men) the Capitalist's and Lord's henchmen—the priests—ensured that the proletariat would never gather enough resolve to revolt. Marx proposed that, if these social injustices were righted, the need to console oneself with religious delusions would evaporate. Of course this did not happen. When Victorian science banished the Christian God from the scene, the vacuum was immediately filled, not by reason, but by the new and far more dangerous secular religions of Communism and National Socialism. Why should this be?

Sigmund Freud produced an answer to this question. He obtained evidence from his clinical practice to show that religion represents only a series of infantile wish fulfillments. Humans are so timid and dependent that, when they have outgrown the protection and solace of their real father, they invent an imaginary Father in heaven to replace him. In Roman Catholicism they also invent a heavenly Mother in the form of the Virgin Mary. In the secular religions of Communism and Fascism they deify a mortal Führer instead. Moreover, human life is burdened by the dread of the death that creeps nearer every day. Life to a materialist is but a moment in annihilation's waste. All men share John Donne's horror at the thought of the wormes will eventually devour them. Andrew Marvell's words lurk uneasily in the recesses of their minds "The grave's a fine and private place. But none I think do there embrace." Furthermore most people are troubled by painful guilt, an emotion as hard to get rid of as the spot on Lady Macbeth's hand. So humans will tend to believe anything that will banish the fear of death and erase the sense of guilt, even if it places us in the power of the priests.

Freud's new psychology also dealt another blow to the philosophy of the Age of Reason. This whole movement was based on the assumption that people order their affairs by the clear light of reason, logic, science and robust common sense. Freud showed that the truth is very different. As Machiavelli had noted before him, (and as economists have only recently discovered) Freud found that people in real life are governed largely by their prejudices and passions—mainly fear, hatred, envy, lust and malice. Recent fMRI brain imaging studies carried out by Drew Western and his colleagues (quoted by Shermer, 2006) have strikingly confirmed this. These scientists did brain scans on subjects given the task of assessing political statements during the 2004 US Presidential election. The scientists expected to see that parts of the brain used in reasoning (dorsolateral prefrontal cortex) would become active. However, that is not what they found: parts of the emotional brain (limbic cortex and ventral striatum) lit up instead. Drew comments that "Essentially, it appears as if partisans twirl the cognitive kaleidoscope until they get the conclusions they want, and then they get massively reinforced for it, with the elimination of negative emotional states and activation of positive ones." In addition Freud gathered mountains of evidence to show that the rational human mind is but a frail barque struggling to stay afloat on the dark and tempestuous sea of unreason known as the Unconscious. The limpid prose of Jane Austen, or the bright paintings of Raphael and Botticelli, may be suitable vehicles to express the workings of the conscious mind. But the writings of Dostoyevski and James Joyce, or, in art the paintings of Goya and Picasso, portray the more powerful machinery of the Id.

As I said earlier the two main props of Western Civilization were faith in reason and the ancient dualist tradition fitted into a modern, rational format by Descartes. The Christian religion formed, as it were, a plaster cast around the developing fragile body of civilization. When the cast was removed the new bones were unhappily found to be still fragile and liable to fracture. Darwin's work in removing the cast was greatly aided by the writings of the philosopher and poet Frederick Nietzsche. He correctly saw that God was dead. By this he meant that Darwin's discoveries had destroyed the credibility of the Christian Church. Although he admired Jesus, who he called "the only Christian", he had a vast contempt for the Christian religion, which he regarded as a series of fantasies that were mainly the creation of St. Paul. Nietzsche called it a religion fit only for slaves (which of course it was since most of the early Christians were in fact Roman slaves). But Nietzsche's solution was unfortunate. The Superman he predicted and advocated formed, alas, the blue print for Fascism.

It is hardly surprising, then, after the ideas promulgated by Darwin, Marx, Freud and Nietzsche had fomented, matured and slowly percolated down from Academia to form the 'common sense' of our times, that the 20th century became the most horrific in human history in which a naked Darwinian struggle for existence, freed from all humanistic constraints, raged between races, between classes, and between cultures, in which super-tyrants flourished on a scale hitherto unknown, and Western Civilization all but perished.

Today the site of the battlefield has abruptly changed. The Age of Reason has returned to Western Europe and to much of the rest of the world. Following the collapse of the Soviet Union, Marxism is no longer a threat. Prospective Supermen tend to land up in the dock at The Hague instead of in a Presidential palace. Material prosperity is spreading slowly but surely throughout the world. But, just as everyone was breathing a sigh of relief, a new and deadly danger has suddenly sprung up out almost nowhere—militant Islam. Islam has, of course, been a threat to Western Civilization, with its Judeo-Christian roots, since the fanatical Arab armies burst out of the desert 1,300 years ago. This threat reached its apogee in the 17th century at the two sieges of Vienna. Since then, Islam declined over the centuries, in Western eyes, into a marginal religion practiced by despised 'natives'. 9/11 changed all that abruptly. But the threat comes, not so much from a Sunni Al-Qaeda intent on restoring the great Caliphate, or from an Iranian Shiite theocracy intent on restoring the lost glories of Darius and Xerxes, but from demographics. Islam has never lost its conviction that it is its manifest duty and destiny to convert, by hook or by crook, the whole world to Islam. Spain, Britain, Italy, Germany, Israel and particularly France now contain sizeable numbers of citizens who are also Muslims. In all these countries the Muslims breed at a much faster rate than do the native population. So it is a Malthusian certainty that these countries, before the end of the century, will have a predominantly Muslim population. Therefore, if these countries are still democracies by that time, it is inevitable they will then become Islamic republics. Threats of this kind usually lead to counter-reactions, just as Fascism was a counter-reaction to Communism. In this case the most important counter-reaction has been the relentless rise of the 'religious right' in the United States. Thus, during the rest of this century most of the world threatens to polarize into an expanded militant Islam (the present Islamic counties plus much of Western Europe) and a militant Christian world (comprised of a mainly Protestant United States and a Catholic Central and South America, and sub-Saharan Africa). History shows that, under such pressure, right-wing regimes tend to develop quasi-fascist tendencies.

So what can the tattered remnants of the supporters of the Enlightenment do in so threatening a situation? This book represents one attempt under this directive. In order to understand our present situation it is necessary to examine in more detail how we got into it. I will examine in particular what truths, if any, are contained in Christianity and in Islam. What can we do to strengthen our ideological defenses against the challenges posed by a newly self-confident and aggressive Islam? To answer this we must examine more carefully the doctrines of the Christianity that used to provide our ideological defence against the hot desert wind of Islam. Modern Biblical scholarship, and the discovery of the Dead Sea Scrolls and the recently discovered lost Gospels including the Gospel of Judas, show that what passes as orthodox Christianity today, both Catholic and Protestant, is mainly the product of theologians and Church leaders working during the three centuries after the death of Jesus. During this period many different Gospels, and versions of what people remembered about what Christ actually said and did, augmented by giving a free rein to a remarkable series of apocryphal fantasies, competed for survival. Can we sift through all this highly dubious extraneous material that official Christianity has accumulated over the centuries, to get back to Christ's original message? One great advantage of Islam is that its theology is much simpler than the Christian theology of the Nicean Creed. No sophisticated person today can believe in the theology that was hammered out by these early Christian committees. A new Reformation is urgently needed. Indeed Thomas Jefferson produced one in his version of the Gospels of the New Testament in which all references to the supernatural were expunged. Even better would be a synthesis of what is rational in the various religions to provide a single system. But I suspect that this would be far outside human capacities to accept, people being what they are.

Then I will examine the present status of the human mind and soul in contemporary science and Western philosophy that lie central to this debate. At the moment this topic is subject to a quasi-religious dogmatism as rigid as any we find in theology. Most neuroscientists and Western philosophers have convinced themselves that it is now a proven scientific fact that the mind and the brain are identical. The question I shall address is whether this is really so, or whether it is yet another example of the human propensity to rely on dogma rather than reason when things get difficult.

In our present dangerous world people are going to believe, if they possibly can, in a system that promises them a life after death instead of annihilation. Given the weakness of human nature, as modern science promises only annihilation, Islam, which promises Paradise, has a great advantage. A culture that teaches that its members are the immortal children of God is in a stronger position over one that says that human life is ordered only by our selfish genes. It is therefore necessary to examine the problem why these scientists adopt this nihilistic position so dogmatically. Their reply is that they are concerned only with the truth and, if it is true that the mind and the brain are identical, and that we are ruled by our selfish genes, then we must simply accept the fact and not whine about it and demean ourselves by chasing after fairy tales. But it is necessary to examine and debate their case critically. This is difficult because most would as soon discuss Ptolemaic epicycles as any dualist theory of mind. But the history of science shows that it is always unwise to refuse even to debate important issues of this kind. In the past scientists have held similar dogmatic notions equally tenaciously that turned out later to be wrong. Besides, the eminent American philosopher Avrum Stroll (2006) in a recent book claims that many problems of this kind are inherently insoluble. He specifically includes the questions of whether God exists and whether human souls survive death. Thus we can hope for more humility from any scientist anxious not further to contribute to the nihilism that is currently undermining civilization.

What counts about a culture is not how it measures against some abstract ideals held sacred by the secular Intelligentsia but whether, in a Darwinian word, it can survive the competition of other cultures. After three centuries of global dominance, the West feels invincible. However, this assurance is based mainly on a (temporary) superior material technology. The Bush administration, in particular, operates on the assumption that the technical and military superiority of the United States allows its Government to pursue an international policy geared almost entirely for the benefit of corporate America with little regard to the feelings and aspirations of other nations, or, indeed, for ordinary folk in America. Its international social policy is limited to the idea that all that needs to be done is to export the American version of democracy, at gunpoint if necessary, around the world. However, the competition today concerns the fate of people's souls, not their pocket books. It might be better to place one's bets on fanatical believers in a militant religion, who are prepared to die gladly for their cause, than on a culture weakened by a nihilism not seen since the days of the collapse of the Roman Empire. It remains to be seen if a Christianity, that most educated people no longer believe in, or a flinty secularism that offers little comfort to the suffering masses, can resist the coming assault.

Introduction. Part 2

I will start this enquiry by asking a number of questions such as: How do people in the West currently relate to the Universe in which they live? Does science explain all that there is to know about the universe and ourselves? What place does, and should, religion play in a world dominated by science? How is the human mind related to the brain and what is the nature of the human soul? What obligations and duties do we have to each other, what are the basic principles of ethics and morality that we should live by and whence do these originate? What are family values? How coherent are the currently dominant ethical themes of racism, sexism and elitism?

I will start with the picture of the world drawn by science and mainstream philosophy today—and then describe what I feel to be wrong with that account. To begin with I will focus on our present concepts of the nature of humans and their place in nature.

The dominant theory in the West on this topic is the biological account of humans as purely material objects produced by the erratic processes of Darwinian evolution. The human mind, including consciousness, is held to be identical with the brain and humans do not possess immortal souls or anything like them. In my previous book 'The Walls of Plato's Cave' I presented, in contrast, a new scientific theory of consciousness and how this relates to its brain. I argued from both a philosophical and a neuroscientific standpoint that the mind and the brain are not identical. The present book explores some repercussions of those arguments and conclusions in the fields of ethics, religion and ideology. My conclusion is that modern neuroscience has become overconfident in reducing human beings to nothing more than biochemical machines and arguing that we now know enough about how the brain works to make any other theory untenable. In contrast, I wish to reopen the age-old question of the human soul—once central to thinking in the civilized world and currently marginalized by science as just a primitive myth.

Modern science has certainly led to great improvements in our material circumstances. In Edwardian times it was hoped that the social and psychological sciences would lead to a parallel improvement in our psychological wellbeing. However, the sorry state of the world today must lead us to inquire why we have failed in this task. Any purely biological account of humans suffers from the disadvantage that biology does not recognize values. In biological Darwinism it is only the survival of an individual's genes that counts. In social Darwinism it is only the survival of the tribe. How then can we defend our humanistic values in a world of fact?

I will review the evidence to show that the contribution over the last two centuries of many of the intelligentsia to civilization has been largely destructive. Born of a fragmentation of knowledge and errors of reasoning, and nurtured by a media addicted to hedonism, violence and sensationalism, their nihilistic doctrines reflect a fatal distortion of the truth about human beings and lead only to an impoverishment of the life of the mind, social ruin and misery—and ultimately formed the road to Auschwitz. As the erstwhile Editor of the *Times*— William Rees-Mogg (1990) said in a leader in *The Independent* "An ignorant and feather brained intelligentsia is a curse of any modern nation, and it is certainly not confined to the United States." My book suggests a new basis for understanding of the meaning of life, and a new basis for civilization, ethics and morality.

FOR VANNA

Myself when young did eagerly frequent
Doctor and Saint and heard great argument
About it and about: but evermore
Came out by the same door as in I went.

Omar Khayyám

CHAPTER 1.

What do you think you are?

Since the dawn of civilization people have sought to discover the nature of their own being—the human body as an object in the physical universe and the human mind that perceives, thinks and feels—the subject in all experience. In previous eras there were many roads to follow in the search for truth. Science discovered facts about the world. Religion, art, music and literature revealed truths about the mind and about human life in all its rich complexity and drama. All these revealed something valid about human nature—about what human beings really are. The appreciation of truth is inseparably an emotional as well as an intellectual experience.

But today powerful voices in science and philosophy are claiming that science represents the *only* route to any kind of truth that is worth having and that the other aspects of human culture have only a secondary value. They claim that cognitive neuroscience will in due course give a complete explanation of all human 'mental' activities in terms of brain mechanisms. We will then be able to give up talking in old fashioned mentalistic terms such as 'perceiving', 'thinking', 'feeling', and 'believing', as well as being able to jettison more general concepts such as 'love', 'beauty', 'values', 'honor', 'justice'—all derided as 'folk psychology'. In their place a mature neuroscience claims to talk about the real things involved, namely physiological functions, such as spiking frequencies in the amygdala and the balance of activity between the prefrontal cortex and the limbic system.

In a similar manner we talk about DNA instead of 'heredity', and about oxidation instead of phlogiston. Thus we should all come to talk in terms of the physical events in our brains that actually constitute, it is alleged, the events that 'folk psychology' expresses in its out-of-date and soon to be superceded vocabulary. This austere doctrine will, this account of science prophesises, explain human activities such as love and hate, devotion and betrayal, art and religion solely in terms of brain mechanisms.

The supporters of this theory of what it means to be human like to present their case as pure science. However, this is not so. This extreme materialism is not the outcome of a purely scientific program but it is the chimerical hybrid of science and a metaphysical theory of mind-brain relationships known as the Identity Theory. This theory simply states that the mind and the brain are identical. However, there is nothing in science itself that leads to this theory although its proponents like to pretend there is. All the scientific evidence (from neuroscience and introspectionist psychology), once deprived of its illegitimate metaphysical underpinnings, indicates rather that both this type of materialism and the Identity Theory are erroneous[1].

The beliefs that humans develop about themselves are not merely a matter of academic concern for philosophers and psychologists. The main course of human conduct springs from the dominant beliefs of the culture concerning human nature: what people come to believe to be the purpose of life, the goals for action, the basis for ethics, morals and values. This book deals with the drastic change in people's beliefs about themselves that has taken place in the last century and with the impact of these changes on politics, ethics and culture that has resulted in our present troubles. The current opinion of the vast majority of contemporary scientists and philosophers is that we are nothing but biochemical machines. One central theme of this book is that this opinion is quite mistaken. It represents the premature jumping to conclusions. We have minds as well as nervous systems.

The work of pioneers in the disciplines of psychology, sociology and political science is constantly liable to perversion by fanatics of the abstract, by creatures of the bureaucracy of limited imagination, less understanding and no compassion, and by people hungry for power, position and prestige. The motive of these pioneers is often not only the selfless pursuit of academic knowledge. They are also enmeshed in the complex hierarchies and politics of Academia. Many are driven by their desire to avenge what they see to be great social and historical wrongs; to protect some sacred 'truth'; and to combat what they see as superstition, ignorance and despair. Alas, history makes blindingly clear that the end result of all their efforts is very often to create even greater wrongs, and to give rise to cultural, economic and political systems based on half-truths and dubious hypotheses. These generate even deeper levels of misery and despair in the unfortunate people caught up, usually against their will, in these ruinous and Utopian schemes for man's salvation.

Among the systems of this type that I will examine are Marxism, the nihilistic theories of Behaviourism and scientific materialism; the myth of the Noble Savage, the newer nihilistic doctrines of people like Wittgenstein, Nietzsche, Heidegger, and Sartre, and all theories that claim that we are *nothing but* naked apes, *nothing but* computers or bundles of reflexes, *nothing but* biophysical mechanisms[2]. I will be using the term 'ideology' throughout this book in the sense of the set of ideas and beliefs that provide the intellectual and moral framework of civilization, the basis for the operations of our culture. The term I would like to use unfortunately does not exist in English, which would be a direct translation of the German 'Weltanschauung'. So 'ideology' will have to do.

Civilizations will collapse if the citizens become alienated and demoralized. Morale depends on ideology, the belief of the citizens that they amount to something, that some purpose is served by all the weary struggle, disappointment and pain of human existence, that their short and anxious lives belong somehow to some greater and nobler whole. If intelligence and reason cannot provide this, then the citizens will seek it somewhere else — in the dark depths of religious and political fanaticism, superstition and tribalism with which, as will be evident to anyone reading any newspaper today, the world is currently awash. As Evelyn Waugh wrote "When people cease to believe in something, they do not believe in nothing. They believe in anything."[3]

Come, fill the Cup, and in the Fire of Spring
The Winter Garment of Repentance fling:
The Bird of Time has but a little way
To fly—and Lo! The Bird is on the Wing.

Omar Khayyám

CHAPTER 2.

Apollonian and Dionysean elements in civilization.

The Age of the Supernatural

In so-called 'primitive' societies the human relationship to supernatural beings hidden behind the natural world is held to be all-important. The myths are accepted by everyone and dominate every aspect of the culture, every aspect of thought and activity. Anthropologists have found that people in such cultures often have an intense sense of belonging to the world, of being at one with nature, an experience of living poetry that renders a life often poor in material aspects nevertheless rich in depths of satisfaction and meaning. This sense of cosmic unity is expressed in ceremony, ritual and sympathetic magic. People feel part of a universe that cares for them. In almost all 'primitive' cultures the supernatural beings that created and sustain the world continue to take an interest in human affairs. In such cultures people believe that they possess immortal souls that survive the death of their bodies to enter another world, the nature of which may or may not depend on the quality of one's acts in this world. But, if the people cease to believe in the myths, cultural collapse rapidly follows, as in the case of the native North Americans following up the opening of America to white settlers. In a few years a proud and effective people were reduced to a pathetic huddle of alcoholics. In this collapse smallpox, the massacre of the buffalo, and the Winchester rifle all played their roles. But the main factor was the contempt shown to them and their beliefs by the all-powerful white invaders.

In more developed societies religions become monotheistic or even, as in the case of Buddhism, atheistic. Nevertheless the supernatural world remains the place where the ultimate meaning of human life on earth is derived. In most religions the concept of some form of existence after the death of the physical body is essential. If that belief is lost, the entire system, including the basis for ethics and morality that it supplies, will be in danger of collapse.

Thus, until recently, the major ideologies of the world were supernatural, based on the concept that life on Earth is played out against the background of another, nobler invisible world. This provided much of the meaning of existence that experience, as poignantly expressed in the Book of Job, teaches us is singularly lacking in the material world. The account of what it is to be human, as described by contemporary biology and psychology, eventually ceases to satisfy many intelligent and sensitive people, or to support them in difficult times. The pursuit of prestige, riches, power and pleasure often eventually leads to painful degrees of disappointment, guilt, fear, ennui and depression. It also tends to promote new and hungry appetites, the inevitable failure to satisfy which leads only to disappointment and resentment. Eventually many people become filled with a sense that their own lives are compounded of futility and they feel adrift without purpose or direction in an unfriendly and alien Cosmos. Of course, many people are fortunately sanguine by nature and manage to live reasonably happy lives even if the walls of civilization are crumbling around them. Such people may be happy to set their horizons on family, work and recreation without a thought to the deeper issues we will be considering here. They really do not care if the respected intelligentsia tell us that we are only automata. But others of more sensitive temperament find this doctrine repellent—especially when applied to those they love. They also bridle at the claim that all human emotions—love, devotion, friendship, compassion, as lived and as expressed in art, music and poetry—are nothing but the antics of nerve nets in their brains. Of course, if this doctrine were really true it would be merely wishful thinking to try and deny it. But I will argue in this book that the doctrine is manifestly false for sound philosophical, biological and cosmological reasons.

Thus one of the main factors that determines whether a civilization will flourish or decay is the power of the ideology shared by its citizens. In other words, what is the answer given by the culture to the all-important question 'What is it all about?' and what is the degree of confidence that we can have that the reply given is true. Can the ideology help people to co-operate harmoniously, to put up with adversity cheerfully, to blend freedom and discipline, to marry selfish and corporate interests and ambitions, to act in a decent, civilized, tolerant and humane manner, while at the same time preventing society from being taken over by its own most ferocious psychopaths and preventing it from falling victim to aggressive and predatory neighbors, or to malignant religious or political fanaticisms? Why do so many civilizations grow, reach a zenith, a golden age, and then enter a period of painful decline leading to extinction? Historians such as Arnold Toynbee[4] who have attempted to answer these questions have not paid sufficient attention to the psychology of these matters.

The Age of Reason

The idea that we could arrive at a valid and satisfactory explanation of the world by reason, or more explicitly by reason linked to observation, hypothesis and experiment that constitutes the method of science, is of very recent vintage, a discovery of the seventeenth century adumbrated by the early Greek scientists, such as Aristarchus of Samos, Democritus and Archimedes. The initial phase of the Age of Reason was distinguished by its optimism. The Renaissance and all the subsequent technological developments and the cultural advances in art, literature, science and philosophy led to a progressive enrichment, both material and psychological, of human life in the West. The political fabric of capitalist democracy, which slowly displaced feudalism during this period, received intellectual expression in the writings of John Locke and Adam Smith. The high tide of optimism and rational content (in the ranks of the intellectuals) with the state of the world was reached at the end of the Eighteenth Century (as mercilessly caricatured by Voltaire in the figure of Dr. Pangloss). People came to believe that they lived in an harmonious and benevolent Cosmos and that they had created a true civilization after centuries of semi-barbarism and religious bigotry. Many intellectuals of the time expressed in their writings the calm and confidence of an Augustan age. People became convinced that reason and scientific progress would solve the remaining problems of human existence. The condition of the poor was certainly unfortunate, but all would be cured by the patient application of reason.

This Augustan age rested squarely on two foundations. The first was the psychological impact of Newton's physics. The discovery of the New World by Columbus antedated by more than a century the discovery of the new Heavens by Galileo. The small static universe of the Middle Ages was replaced by the first glimmering understanding of the tremendous stellar Universe as we now know it. In this transition, the reassuring sense of cosmos rather than the terrifying sense of chaos was maintained by Newton's discoveries. 'God said Let Newton be! and all was light'[5]. Newton's cosmology described a vast heavenly machine that worked with perfect precision and harmony all in obedience to a few simple Laws of Nature. Contemplation of so noble a cosmological edifice induced in Newton's contemporaries a sense of reverent awe that spilled over into their ideology. The Newtonian ideas of harmony, balance and proportion reinforced the swell of such ideas and values that came from the rediscovery of classical Greek and Roman sculpture, architecture, writing, science and philosophy. As Bullard (1972) has put it:

"The eighteenth-century world picture of an ideal universe and an ideal society, each running of themselves as a mechanism, a clock, almost a logical construct, strangely mirrors Newton's work on the motion of the planets... ...In our own day the successes of physics, the discovery of worlds packed within worlds like Chinese boxes and all the gadgets and inventions that have flowed from the knowledge has given us a feeling of omnipotence where any failure or distress, poverty, illness or unhappiness is thought of as an intolerable and unnecessary failure of the system of society."

Vestiges of this attitude are still to be found today. A vivid example is to be found in the diary of Admiral Richard E. Byrd (1939) in which he expresses the belief that the transcendental purpose of human existence comes from an aesthetic response to the world's strange beauty and not from reason, which has, he claimed, to be transcended. Our present task is to bring reason and our feeling for the world into line.

The great flowering of European civilization in the eighteenth and nineteenth centuries was made possible by the combination of Newtonian cosmology, and the attitude of mind that this induced, with Cartesian psychology, which was the second founding stone of Western civilization. This combination allowed people to believe, on the basis of reason rather than faith, that they lived in a universe specially created for them by a Creator, whose concern for harmony, balance and proportion was guaranteed by Newton's physics, and whose love and concern for the human race was guaranteed by the message that the great religious leaders brought to earth. The existence of the human soul, which is required for this system to work, was accounted for by Cartesian psychology and philosophy, which stated, on basis of reason not faith, that we are composed of a material body and an immaterial mind. This combination gave people the basic confidence that allowed political democracy to develop in England following the Glorious Revolution of 1688 and in the United States following the revolution of 1776. It also underwrote the great developments in science, art, literature and music characteristic of these centuries. One might say, for example, that Beethoven's music, particularly the ninth Symphony, was the ultimate expression in art of an optimistic faith in a just and reasonable Cosmos. The fine optimism of the age was, however, confined almost entirely to the aristocracy and the bourgeoisie and their philosophers, which is not surprising, as the bulk of the proletariat did not know how to write. The history of the twentieth century may be written in terms of the rapid decay and collapse of this system and its replacement by the monstrous aberrations that infest our world today.

Except for militant Islam and a few remote tribes, there is only one culture[6] in the world today. Western scientific culture (including until quite recently its pathological aberration Marxism) has engulfed and overwhelmed all the rest including the once great civilizations of the East as well as innumerable small cultures around the world. In today's world, science, together with fraudulent imitations of science, are dominant in directing human thought and affairs. Against a background of history and prehistory lasting millions of years, four hundred years of science have totally altered the conditions of human life and death on this planet, together with people's estimate of their own place in nature. The structure of modern physical and biological science is humanity's greatest intellectual achievement. It has totally transformed almost every aspect of daily life. But it contains the seeds of a mortal danger.

The physical and biological sciences have acted mainly for the good on human material circumstances. But what about the impact of science, in particular psychology and the social sciences, on human *psychological* circumstances? Unfortunately here the picture is bleaker. For a short period in history it was widely believed that science might achieve in the social and psychological fields results comparable to its success in the physical and biological spheres. H.G. Wells gave an imaginative expression of these yearnings in his novels *The Shape of Things to Come* and *Men like Gods*. The brilliant successes of the physical sciences from Newton to Einstein and of the medical sciences from Harvey to Lister, led in late Victorian and Edwardian times to hopes that psychology and sociology might have equally brilliant futures in the eradication of poverty, violence, crime, war, oppression, tyranny and other social ills. The carnage of the First World War put an abrupt end to all that. The failure to attain these goals can hardly be denied today. Of course an attitude of unremitting gloom would be equally unrealistic. Life at the material level for most Westerners is vastly better today than in Edwardian times. But life at the psychological level is not. Waugh's "deep healing draughts of Edwardian certainty" have gone forever. The last decades have seen a steady rise in all manner of indices of social and psychological ill health and a general sour sleaziness all too obvious in many aspects of modern life, in particular in politics, the media and the arts. One objective of applied science should be to make the world a better place to live in. Why, then, have the social sciences so singularly failed in their task?

All human societies operate to satisfy basic human needs, some purely biological, others psychological. These include such things as the desire for prestige, love and attention; the need for understanding and enlightenment; the imperative to cope with the most powerful of human emotions—hatred, envy, jealousy and the thirst for revenge; the social imperative to belong to some type of group, and so on. Some people wish above all to achieve harmony and contentment; others look for stimulation and excitement; all seek to avoid grief, misery, boredom and despair. These complex psychological needs generate the appropriate social structures, rules and norms to meet and contain them. For example, the hardest burden that we have to bear—bereavement—will be eased by a culture that enables us somehow to come to terms with the loss and to cope with the pain; and by a psychosocial structure which provides a practical programme to attain these ends.

Our present troubles arise, I suggest, for five reasons.

(1) The infant science syndrome. The initial stages of a science are often marked by a series of false starts of a more or less bizarre character. Chemistry, after all, grew out of alchemy; astronomy from astrology; and modern medicine developed out of the astonishing and lethal systems of the eighteenth

century, in which bleeding and purging were responsible for the deaths of swathes of patients. In some of these false starts, development is distorted by some desperate human need that forces short cuts in the search for knowledge. In alchemy it was the lust for gold and the fear of death; in astrology the wish to see into the future; in early medicine the need to do *something* to relieve suffering and prevent death; in Marxism it was the wretched state of the Victorian poor. The essence of the scientific method is the construction of hypotheses to explain the data. It is essential to realize that these hypotheses are always limited and provisional and may be revised or abandoned at any time in the light of new evidence or the advent of a better theory. This the infant social sciences have spectacularly failed to do. Dying theories are defended to the death.

(2) The application of social science at any stage to the solution of human problems leads at once to practical politics. Some people will benefit from the application of the particular social theory; others are likely to be the losers. Both will be motivated to distort the truth for their own ends. The role of the Soviet apparatchiks in resisting democratic and capitalist reform is an example. The curious belief of the governments of the United States and the United Kingdom that the way to improve health care is by swelling the health bureaucracy is another.

(3) In any enterprise of this kind there is always the danger that the *reductionist factor* will take over. This leads the over-enthusiastic proponents of the new scheme to save mankind, as the new theory often becomes in the hands of its fanatical supporters, to extend the scope of the theory to wider and wider fields over and above the one into which it was first introduced—social realism in art, Lysenkoism[7] in biology and fictitious psychoanalytical interpretations of almost everything are examples.

(4) Any revolution claiming to be based on humanitarian ideals and benevolent science, so worthy as to permit violence in the struggle to implement them, is likely to be hijacked by

terrorists such as Robespierre, Lenin, Stalin, Mao, Pol Pot and Asama Bin Laden.

(5) The *metaphysical factor*. All science is based on what Burtt (1932) termed a series of metaphysical assumptions and what Broad (1923) called Basic Limiting Principles. The scientist usually takes these as being self-evidently true and indeed rarely thinks about them at all. However, these are only assumptions, even if justifiable in the particular circumstances of the time, and not absolute truths. An example is the dogma that people can only obtain or exchange information by use of one of the recognized channels of sense. This assumption makes telepathy impossible, so any experimental evidence that telepathy exists will be rejected for this metaphysical reason.

To summarize: we can analyze our present problems in ideology under the five headings I have outlined: 'Infant Science', 'Practical Politics', 'Reductionism', 'Hijacking' and the 'Metaphysical'.

The political events of an era are functions of underlying, almost undetected, stresses and changes in ideology, just as the formation of crevasses and seracs on the surface of a glacier are functions of the slow movement of the ice underneath. Our task here, as it were, is to try and discern the movements of the ice under the turmoil of surface events. There is usually a long delay between the events that lead to changes in ideology and the actual expression of these changes in the cultural and political life of the epoch. For example, the seventeenth century saw the germinal work of Galileo, Newton, Locke and Hobbes: at the same time it saw the last of the savage religious wars in Europe involving differences in doctrine that were to become totally unimportant one hundred years later, by when educated people had diverted their attention form religion to science.

The Romantic Revival

Rousseau

Human beings are rarely content with what they have and are constantly seeking something different[8]. The Age of Reason provided a respite from the terrible religious wars of the seventeenth century that reduced much of Germany to a charnel house. But harmony and calm were no sooner attained than restless people became dissatisfied and looked around for something more exciting and glamorous. Moreover, the great Lisbon earthquake of 1755 caused many people to lose their faith in a benign cosmos. Many of the intelligentsia became disenchanted with the authoritarian structure of European society and with the privileges and arrogance of the ruling classes, and they looked for a way to put these wrongs to right. Both groups found what they wanted in the writings of Rousseau.

Jean Jacques Rousseau was a native of Switzerland, in whose memory there is still a little park on an island in the middle of the Rhône in Geneva. He suffered greatly from mental instability all his life, including a serious attack of paranoia in 1767-1768. The experiences of his unhappy childhood resulted in his psychopathic personality and a disorderly life, during which he placed his own children in a foundlings' home and fought bitterly with all his friends[9]. But it also left him with the passionate belief that man is born good and is only made evil by the miserable circumstances of his life, by the sick society into which he is born. He felt it was absurd to claim that the actions of people and the tone of the culture should be set by reason alone. What people *felt*, felt deeply and passionately, were much more important for him than all the dusty writings of the philosophers of reason. Thus Rousseau was largely responsible for two movements of immense importance in the further development of Western civilization—the Romantic political movements and the cult of the 'Noble Savage'.

Christian doctrine has always been that man is born in sin and has to struggle to become good. Other religions teach much the same. Machiavelli (1970) put it thus: "All writers on politics have pointed out, and throughout history there are plenty of examples which indicate, that in constituting and legislating for a commonwealth it must needs be taken for granted that all men are wicked and that they will always give vent to the malignity that is in their minds when opportunity offers...men never do good unless necessity drives them to it..."

Rousseau reversed this with his dictum 'Man is born free but everywhere is in chains'. At about this time the first reports of explorers from Tahiti were reaching Europe and seemed at the time to represent a striking confirmation of Rousseau's views. The beautiful, seductive islanders, who had never had to work for a living, so bountiful was Nature, were clearly Noble Savages.

Rousseau has, however, to some extent been misinterpreted by his critics and enemies (Dent, 1988). He never claimed that *all* society is evil; rather he picked out certain elements of society as causing particular damage. He did not object to social regulation based on mutual agreements between equals. He said that man is good until he is subjected to, or controlled by, the domineering will of another, and especially after he has been treated with contempt by others with an inflamed *amour propre* (sense of their own importance) as Rousseau himself must have had to endure so many times in his own life. Rousseau particularly disliked universities and higher learning in general, which he saw all too often as leading to disabling doubts, and as making a mock of common beliefs that sustain ordinary human action[10]. Academics, in his view, strive mainly for prestige, power and celebrity, a view given graphic expression in our day in the novels of C.P. Snow. He admired Bacon, Descartes and Newton, for example, who he felt had earned their honor and esteem. But celebrity that leads to an attitude of disdainful superiority towards others, such as that expressed recently by some prominent scientists towards parapsychologists, is always bad. "It is true that in France Socrates would not have drunk the hemlock, but he would have drunk a potion infinitely more bitter, of insult, mockery and contempt a hundred times worse than death." (Rousseau, 1973). At times he had very sound instincts. He taught that law and government are largely corrupt because they legalize robbery and abuse; and one might add they fight wars too. Of course some systems of government are inherently more corrupt than others; in a democracy one can always kick the rascals out[11]. Rousseau also had the very sound insight that reforming civil institutions will not set society aright; this can only be done by changing men's souls:

> "...everything being reduced to appearance, there is nothing but art and mummery in every honor, friendship, virtue and vice itself...we have nothing to show for ourselves but a frivolous and deceitful appearance, honor without virtue, reason without wisdom, and pleasure without happiness"[12].

This fits our own times, in which the 'image makers' and 'spin doctors' play so large a role, like a glove.

However, Rousseau's definition of 'natural' as 'good' is frankly circular, since the natural is defined as that which is good—that which makes for growth and a secure and rich life, which abuts on his claim that the good is natural to humans.

The new Romantic movement that flowered amongst the intelligentsia in the early and middle years of the nineteenth century had a potent and beneficial effect on the arts as personified, for example by Byron, Wagner and Turner. The eighteenth century ideals of harmony, balance and proportion (think of Addison, Mozart and the influence of Palladio) were thrown out of the window (by people like Shelley, Byron and Wagner) and were replaced by Dionysean ideals of emotional extravagance in place of quiet contentment, of extremism in place of moderation and restraint, and full license to biological instincts in place of self-discipline and self-control. Thus makes for splendid art, but the application of such ideas to practical living and politics leads to disaster. Romantic political movements usually lead to tyranny, either of the left or of the right[13], and to a resurgence of tribal patterns of behaviour that lie at the roots of so much of modern evil. The survival of civilization depends on the steadfast defense by individual people at all levels of the Apollonian values of true civilization and the refusal to be seduced by glamorous but ultimately ruinous schemes for salvation as offered, for example, by Fascist and Communist parties. Unfortunately many of the intelligentsia, especially in the Thirties, failed to follow this advice.

For example, Sydney and Beatrice Webb were leading lights of the British intelligentsia in the period between the wars and were to a large extent responsible for the later development of the Labour Party and its pre-Blair doctrines. Their book *Soviet Communism: A New Civilization* was based entirely on the text of the Soviet constitution, which every child knows had nothing to do with the realities of Soviet life and politics. Their book is, alas, pure fiction, and might be regarded merely as a sad monument to the mistaken endeavors of two worthy innocents most earnest to do good. However, contemporary evidence (Flew, personal communication) indicates that the Webbs were not just naive but actually knew what was going on during Stalin's great terror, and did not care! They shrugged it off according to Robespierre's thesis of eggs and omelets. Bertrand Russell records in his autobiography (1948): "Both of them were fundamentally undemocratic, and regarded it as a function of a statesman to bamboozle or terrorize the populace". It is amazing that it has taken nearly a century for the people of Eastern Europe to throw off the legacy of this attitude so clearly manifested by the elite of the Communist system. One can only hope that contemporary followers of the Webbs elsewhere will follow suit.

It may be no coincidence that many of the early socialists were by profession writers of fiction (such as Wells, Shaw, Day Lewis and many others). Others, such as G.D.H. Cole, wrote novels for a hobby. Socialism and Communism rest on a series of romantic myths or fantasies, such as the idea that tinkering with social systems is the way to improve human life—instead of following Rousseau's prescription about the need to change individual souls; or the idea that a capitalist class in a democracy is likely to oppress and exploit the people more than a communist elite does. This has been shown to be historically untrue in every country where it has been put to the test. Another socialist delusion is that the concept of 'public ownership of the means of production' is any more than vacuous nonsense. There is nothing 'public' about a swollen and sullen bureaucracy, and the people enjoy no 'ownership', in any meaningful sense of this term, of a State monopoly. Socialism errs fatally by confusing the State and the people. Fascism, in part, represented the romantic attempt to recreate the lost splendours of the Roman Empire with all its brutal ruthlessness, or, in the case of Hitler's Germany, the prehistoric glitter of the Herrenvolk.

During most of the nineteenth century the developing fury of the Dionysean world view stayed mainly within the confines of the arts, and only touched on politics in the form of seedy little bands of conspirators congregating in the shadows in the coffee houses of Europe. However, the attitudes and impulses generated by these powerfully evocative writers and artists were to bear bitter fruit in the next century. Of course, some of the practical results of the teachings of the great Romantics were beneficial. Before Rousseau, for example, no one took much notice of the Alps, which were regarded as cold, useless and dangerous. This is possibly why the very Apollonian Swiss named the park after him in Geneva, since they could hardly have approved of his political doctrines. But the incitement to surrender oneself to tumultuous emotions, to forgo self-discipline in favor of doing one's own thing come what may, to submerge oneself in an impassioned herd, neglected to take into account the terrible nature of the collectively generated sadism, hatred and paranoia that may result and that surfaced, for example, in the Coliseum in Rome, in the Nuremberg rallies, in a minor but significant form in the person of James Bond and all that he stands for in terms of cultural decadence; and, in a coldly intellectual manifestation, in the higher reaches of the KGB. The romantic political intelligentsia brought back to life dangerous social instincts—throwbacks to the days when men in packs hunted other men over the land left by the retreating glaciers in Europe. After the bloody explosion that results the intelligentsia are singularly slow to see the connection between their writings and the holocaust. Would Hitler's takeover of Germany have been so easy without the previous writings of Hegel, Fichte and Rousseau advocating the Totalitarian State, of Nietszche and Wagner praising cruelty, war and the Superman, of the social Darwinists preaching that the race goes to the strong, ruthless and cunning? Was the Communist take over aided by the nihilist philosophers and scientists who claimed that people are things, mere mindless automata, computers made of meat? Extolling the virtues of a Super Cause is just as dangerous as extolling the virtues of a Superman.

Hegel

Allies in the process of destroying civilization are to be found in those members of the intelligentsia who attack the basic elements of the system of ideas on which civilization is based without putting anything adequate in their place. These allies do not have to be romantic extremists themselves. Nor do they actually have to teach that people are just mindless automata, or just bundles of reflexes and instincts, or that the universe is ruled by blind chance and blind chance alone. Anyone can see that such biased, distorted, misguided and extreme opinions are unlikely to do civilization much good, even if they had any semblance of being true, which they do not. But, of course, by the end of the twentieth century we have at least learned that propaganda will substitute for truth any day. The damage can be done by much subtler means than that. An example of this category of the Intelligentsia is Hegel. In his devastating critique of Hegel as a political philosopher[14], Popper (1962) makes the case that Hegel was not the first, nor the last, of a long line of Party hacks concerned with the promotion of a totalitarian society. Popper suggests that Hegel was primarily concerned with giving academic respectability to the absolutist and totalitarian ideas of his master and patron, Frederick William III of Prussia. He did this in a most subtle and ingenious a manner. One way he could have chosen would have been to write a series of books simply putting forward in a robust and straightforward fashion the Totalitarian position, which after all can be argued in an intelligible manner, as indeed Plato himself did in the *Republic*. Hegel, however, did something else and that was to create a philosophical system couched in the densest and most impenetrable language that gives the appearance of enormous profundity and scholarship, but which in fact is almost totally devoid of meaning. The effect on the reader, particularly on someone reading the original German, is to make him accept the totalitarian propaganda for reasons he thinks he understands, but which he actually does not. Much of the illusion depends on the unfortunate structure of the German language—it is much harder to get away with this sort of thing in French! Hegel's writings are essentially meaningless verbiage, but they have a powerful, almost magical, power of suggestion and literary hypnosis on the earnest and naïve reader not familiar with con games of this degree of subtlety and boldness. Hegel's nonsense, of course, forms the basis of communist theory[15]. Reichenbach (1971) comments on this sort of thing:

> "But darkness of language has too often been the guise of a philosophy of trivialities mingled with falsehood and nonsense—whether it teaches the identity of opposites, the doctrine that contradiction is the root of motion and life, or the concept that nothing is something".

This applies to many modern philosophers besides Hegel as we will see, in particular to Hegel's principle heir—Karl Marx.

Karl Marx

Darwin's correct and morally neutral scientific theory

that only the fit survive nevertheless unfortunately invites interpretation in the realm of human affairs by ambitious social engineers, such as Karl Marx, of 'fit' as 'strong, ruthless and cunning'. Marx himself was a man consumed by spite, envy and hatred. His venom was concentrated mainly on his great rival in the International Socialist movement Lasalle, a much better man by far in every way than Marx. In particular Marx's virulent anti-Semitism focused on Lasalle's Jewishness. Marx frequently referred to Lasalle in his letters to Engels as "that Jewish nigger". Marx treated everyone, except possibly his own family, with the utmost contempt, deviousness and malice[16]. It is not hard to see why he advocated class warfare, rather than class reconciliation, as the solution of human problems. Marx used the state of the poor in England during the Industrial Revolution merely as an excuse to project his own venomous personality onto the world stage. He wished to destroy the bourgeoisie, for reasons welling out of his own psychopathology, and he knew well how to recruit and inflame the native resentment and envy of others in order to bring about his goal. Unlike Hitler, he was unable to put his own doctrines into action. His disciples Lenin, Stalin and Mao did that for him.

Frederick Nietzsche

A variant on the theme of the Noble Savage is provided by Nietzsche. He did not extol the virtues of imaginary Noble Savages but of real feudal warriors instead. Nietzsche came from a mundane middle class background and was raised in an entirely female household with no male figure. He found human contacts very difficult all his life and his only real friend was his devoted sister. He never married and lived most of his life flitting between boarding houses and cheap hotels in Lombardy and the Engadine—solitary, shy, vulnerable and eccentric. It is easy to see why he became a timid bookworm, terrified of women. In compensation he developed a rich fantasy life passionately admiring everything he was not, especially forceful, ruthless aristocrats like Cesare Borgia, and noble rebels, such as Byron.

His philosophy is dominated by wish-fulfilling fantasies. His impact is due simply to the fact that he was a great writer and had the gift of expressing his searing emotions in powerful poetry. He expounded the philosophy of the Superman—that is, Machiavelli's portrait of Cesare Borgia. Nietzsche openly extolled the virtues of war and the ruthless suppression of the weak. His philosophy proved very useful to the Fascists of the following century. His views also dominated the young group of fanatical Serbian nationalists led by Gavrilo Princip, who assassinated the Archduke Franz Ferdinand at Sarajevo. Princip always kept by him this quotation from Nietzsche

> I know whence I arrive
> Unsatisfied like the flame
> I glow and writhe
> Everything I embrace becomes light
> Everything that I leave becomes coal
> Flame I am surely.

During feudal times waging war was the principle, if not the only, function of the aristocracy. Nietzsche felt that this was only right, and he taught that war, with its bravery and brio, was the highest form of human endeavor. This view was also expressed by Mussolini, and by Conan Doyle in his historical novels *Sir Nigel* and *The White Company*. Nietzsche regarded the Christian model for human behaviour, and its theoretical dislike of war, with the greatest contempt. He thought it a religion fit only for slaves, and that Christianity had stifled the brave and worthy model that the Greeks had epitomized.

Wagner's philosophy, as well as his operas, which were only one part of his grandiose philosophy, urged a return to the value system of the tribal Germans. Barzun (1950) has argued that Nietzsche's writings, together with those of Wagner, paved the way for the First World War as well as for Hitler. He traces the boiling hostilities and resentments that consumed the peoples of Europe during the fifty years prior to 1914 to the rhetoric of

Marx, Wagner and Nietzsche, together with Herbert Spencer's social interpretation of Darwinian evolutionary theory. These four currents of malignancy, Barzun suggests, combined to cause the disastrous explosions of 1914, 1917 and 1933, from which we are only now painfully and slowly recovering.

A similar conclusion is drawn by Frederic Morton in "Thunder at Twilight"—his account of the events that led up to the First World War. Morton quotes some very respectable people who were carried away by this madness. For example, Sigmund Freud said in 1914 "There is a crisis in the air...may it soon explode so that the air is clear." The poet Alfred Walter Heymel wrote:

"In the wealth of peace we feel the deadliest dread.
We are bereft of prowess, mission, or direction,
And long and cry for war."

In art the Futurist manifesto exalted war because it would blow away the stultification of present concepts and structures. Adolf Hitler was only expressing a widely held emotion when he said in *Mein Kampf*—

"The sense of approaching catastrophe turned at last to longing: let heaven finally give reign to the fate that could no longer be thwarted. And then the first mighty lightening flash struck the earth: the storm was unleashed, and with the thunder of heaven there mingled the roar of the World War batteries."

Such is the effect of an overdose of Wagner and Nietzsche on an unbalanced mind.

My term 'The myth of the Noble Savage' should not be misinterpreted so as to imply that some 'savages' may not be in fact noble. As I said in the previous Chapter, people in preliterate cultures often are noble, but they are so because of the moral aspects of their culture. They are not noble *because* they are savages. Rousseau and his followers assumed that savages are noble by *nature*. Whereas the fact is that they are noble by virtue of their sophisticated cultures. Noble savages are born potential ignoble savages, honed by evolution, as are the rest of us. Some savages stayed ignoble because of their ignoble cultures. For example the Aztecs practised human sacrifice and the Caribs were cruel cannibals. Others, such as the Hopi and the Tibetans, attain nobility because their cultures are noble.

More on the Noble Savage: Mead and Freeman

The myth of the noble savage is still very much alive and is of paramount importance in guiding 'progressive' ideas of how to bring up and educate children, as well as in the area of many social and political concepts such as 'natural justice' and 'human rights'. Rousseau may have done much to create the myth but its current power owes more to the anthropological school of Franz Boas and to its star—Margaret Mead. Her *Coming of Age in Samoa* (1928) has had an enormous influence, and has widely been regarded as providing hard, scientific evidence to support the theory of the Noble Savage. It will be recalled that Margaret Mead portrays Samoa as an earthly paradise where love, sex, ambition, child rearing, adolescence, politics, etc. are all conducted in the most Apollonian manner—relaxed, calm with the minimum of stress and discord, very little neurosis or religious sentiment, acceptance of free love—the very epitome of all that the most humane of liberal and cultured post-Freudian human beings could possibly hope for.

It came, therefore, as a severe shock to many people to discover that this earthly paradise existed only in Margaret Mead's imagination. The devastating critique of her work by the anthropologist Derek Freeman in his two books *Margaret Mead and Samoa* (1983) and *The Fateful Hoaxing of Margaret Mead (1999)* leaves no shadow of any possible doubt that she was guilty of a whole series of the most heinous scientific errors. Freeman disclosed that she had spent only ten months in Samoa; she could not speak Samoan; she lived with a non-Samoan family and had only tenuous contacts with the Samoan people. She talked mainly to teenagers through an interpreter and Freeman decided that they were mostly pulling her leg. She had been sent out to Samoa by Franz Boas with the strong (no doubt unconscious) ambition of providing data to confirm Boas's hypothesis of the overriding importance of cultural factors (nurture) in determining human behaviour and culture, as opposed to the role of inheritance (nature), whose predominance was asserted by the Eugenics school with whom Boas was in bitter conflict at the time. Freeman has carried out extensive fieldwork in Samoa and he produces abundant evidence that the Samoan people are quite different in every respect from the creations of Mead's fertile imagination. She believed strongly in the myth of the Noble Savage and what she believed *a priori* determined what she recorded in her book, rather than what even the most cursory examination of the facts would have revealed to anyone who had any glimmering of a notion of how an anthropological field study ought to be carried out. The Samoan culture is actually extremely hierarchical, very tense, full of conflict and neurosis, with a very puritanical religion and extremely conservative views about sex. There is no evidence that Mead was a conscious cheat or fraud. She was merely inexperienced, idealistic and naïve—not the first graduate student to be hoodwinked by her mentor.

It is difficult to over-estimate the harm done by this myth. Humans are actually the outcome of millions of years of Darwinian evolution where only the ability to survive counts. This requires character traits the opposite in almost every respect from those attributed by the myth to the Noble Savage. Anything noble about twentieth century humans has been derived from learning, from their own unceasing toil and painful struggle to create and defend the values of civilization against the so-called law of the jungle, and from the great individual human ethical teachers such as Socrates, Moses, the historical Jesus, the anonymous authors of the Upanishads and Prince Gautama. Children are in the main born Hobbesian savages and have to be taught civilized values and behaviour. Hence the counter claim that all we have to do in child rearing is to allow the child to develop 'naturally', to develop his or her personality and 'creativity' with the minimum of interference, is liable to increase the number of ignoble savages, delinquents and yobs in the population, as the nature of many of the products of the comprehensive schools in Britain, where the myth of the Noble Savage still holds sway amongst the 'progressive' teachers, makes plain. I am not in any way recommending a return to Stoic ideals of Thomas Arnold and the system of education based on fear and repression that he originated. Education must be based on the constant active instillation of humanistic values and not on the mistaken belief that these will evolve 'naturally'. The American traitor John Walker is the ultimate expression of the cult of the Noble Savage. His parents, and the hedonistic subculture into which he was born, failed to provide him with any guide lines for the building of his character and left it all to nature with catastrophic results.

Once upon a time, by all accounts, there really was a tribe of Noble Savages—gentle, beautiful and kind. They were called Arawaks and lived in the West Indies. Those that were not eaten by the Caribs were exterminated amongst scenes of hideous brutality by the Christian Spaniards.

The Age of Nihilism

Heidegger and Sartre

The collapse of the optimistic ethical word view of the West (to use Schweitzer's phrase) following the dreadful and senseless carnage of World War I led rapidly to a general attitude of cynicism and despair. This was fed into philosophy in particular by the existentialists led by Heidegger and Sartre. There could hardly be a greater contrast, in style but not in content, between the archpriests of Existentialism, Martin Heidegger and Jean-Paul Sartre. Everything they wrote derived from the conviction they shared that not only do people not have immortal souls, but also the Self does not exist either. A person, in other words, is just a bundle of his or her attributes and acts. Heidegger writes in such an obscure and dense style that it is very easy to feel that most of what he says is totally meaningless, and, the more we struggle to wade through the verbiage, the stronger this feeling becomes. Take a hard look at a typical Heidegger (1958) aphorism "'Time' is called the first name of the truth of Being, and this truth is the presence of Being and thus Being itself."—splendid hieratic prose, no doubt, but does it make any sense?[17]

By contrast, Sartre has an elegant, limpid, down-to-earth style reminiscent of Descartes. His definition of consciousness is "...a being, the nature of which is to be conscious of the nothingness of its being". He denied the existence of the Self on the grounds that if there was one it could only be an immediate state of consciousness experienced just like any other state of consciousness (which it obviously isn't); or else it must be something other than a state of consciousness that merely unifies all the states of consciousness into one coherent entity, since all states of consciousness would be ontologically distinct from what I am (Ellis, 1986). These theories all derive ultimately from Hume's claim that, whenever he searched around in his consciousness for a 'Self' he could never find one, only his own sensations, images and thoughts. The answer to this, of course, is to ask, as did Kant, what agent was doing the searching.

Heidegger (1962) denied that the Self exists on the grounds that—

> "I am my world of interests and concerns, my living biography...I am my hopes, fears, aspirations, ideals and cynicisms...I am the 'me' that my friends know with their expectations of how I look and what I might do...I am the living centre of my experiencing, of my concerns, interests and activities."

He taught that in ordinary life—the domain of *das Man*—we are unconscious of our own existence and we need to experience anguish to become conscious of ourselves. Man's miserable, forlorn existence, for which he never asked, is terminated by

death and leads to nothingness. But we can participate in the
world and have companions and be oriented towards the future.
We have to transcend ourselves out of Nothingness towards
Being by taking resolute decisions and arrest our destiny by a
communion with the earth and world. Contrast this gloomy and
negative attitude towards the Self with Barrett's (1986) theory of
the 'Concrete' Self—"the I that lives and breathes in intimacy
with its own body, enmeshed in memories, anxious about death,
and possibly hoping, if it dare, for some kind of salvation and it
is free, no mere product of human nature, and external stimuli."
This clearly derives from Berkeley:

> "How often must I repeat, that I know or am conscious
> of my own being; and that I myself am not my ideas,
> but somewhat else, a thinking active principle that
> perceives, knows, will and operates about ideas. I know
> that...I am therefore one individual principle, distinct
> from colour and sound; and, for the same reason, free
> from all other sensible things and inert ideas."

Sartre likewise complained about the 'absurdity of human
life, man's gnawing anguish, his solitude, and his alienation'
and he was perversely attracted only to the dreariness and
emptiness that life on this earth, devoid of any transcendental
vision, is likely to bring. Salvation for Sartre (1957) can only be
reached by totally committed strivings towards a goal—that is
by fanaticism.

> "Man is nothing else but what he makes of himself.
> There is no reality except in action...Man is nothing
> else than his plan; he exists only to the extent that he
> fulfills himself; he is therefore nothing else than the
> ensemble of these acts, nothing else than his life."

It is sad that the 'resolute decisions' recommended by
Heidegger only led to his becoming a life-long Nazi; and the
goals that Sartre strove for most of his life were those provided

by the Communist Party. After the war an attempt was made by an influential group of Heidegger's followers in Paris to cover up the extent of his involvement with the Nazis. They pretended that he was only a Party member for a few months around 1933 and that his motive was to protect his students. But evidence has come to light recently in Germany (Zimmerman, 1989) that shows that Heidegger was an enthusiastic Party member right up to 1945 and that he saw himself as the *Eminence Grise* of National Socialism. Sartre turned away from Communism only in 1956, following the repression of the Hungarian revolt. But the Angka Leu group, including Pol Pot, in Cambodia, who were the intellectuals behind the Khmer Rouge, were all francophone followers of Sartre who had spent many years in Paris. They applied his doctrine of 'necessary violence' in the killing fields. Rorty (1989) concedes that Heidegger, for all that he was one of the century's most original thinkers, happened to be a pretty nasty character. But Rorty also claims that this is unimportant on the grounds that the philosophical importance of a thinker is entirely independent of that person's moral worth. This may be so in the case of scientists such as Newton, who was also a pretty unpleasant character (but not on the scale of Heidegger!), or pure logicians, but it is emphatically not so in the case of philosophers who take a 'global' outlook on humanity and its nature and goals and who, as Paul Johnson (1988) puts it, take it upon themselves to tell us how to live our lives: or, even if they do not go as far as that, nevertheless make statements that will affect the way that their readers will look at their own lives and actions.

Wittgenstein

The paralyzing effect that Hegel's nonsense had upon Continental philosophy was achieved by much the same means in the case of British philosophy by Ludwig Wittgenstein, but for quite different reasons. Wittgenstein was no party hack but there is a possibility based on evidence supplied to me by Canon C.E. Raven, who was Vice-Chancellor of Cambridge University at the time that Wittgenstein was Professor of Philosophy there, and by A.J. Ayer, who know him well, to show that he may have suffered at the end of his life from a type of schizoid disturbance marked by episodes of paranoia. Canon Raven told me that he often had difficulty in contacting Wittgenstein, who was in the habit of hiding from his imaginary enemies in surrounding villages. This, however, did not amount to a fully developed form of schizophrenia. Fitzgerald and Berman (1994) recount that Professor Norman Moore of Dublin treated Wittgenstein for depression and did not find any signs of schizophrenia. So it is likely that Wittgenstein suffered from a depressive illness with episodes of paranoia (if Canon Raven did not invent his story which I can see no reason to suppose that he did). Some schizophrenics show a subtle form of thought disorder known as 'schizophrenese'. This is a form of remarkably powerful poetry that some schizophrenics and near schizophrenics can write and speak. Its emotional and hypnotic power is generated by the fact that connections between phrases and ideas come to be dominated by archetypal and paralogical associations in place of the dry logic of ordinary prose. But you do not have to be a schizophrenic to be able to write schizophrenese. James Joyce is a case in point. He himself was not schizophrenic although he was certainly very schizoid and his daughter developed the full illness. *Ulysses* is a work of genius written in English. *Finnegan's Wake* is a work of genius written in schizophrenese. I suggest that Wittgenstein was clinically very similar to Joyce — never actually schizophrenic but capable of writing schizophrenese.

Wittgenstein himself said that philosophy ought to be written as a 'poetic composition'. He also said that he could only express himself in aphorisms and he found it impossible to construct any longer works. In the 1950s I spent two years at Cambridge as a graduate student in psychology and I used to attend the weekly meetings of the disciples of the Master, as they obviously regarded themselves, led by John Wisdom. I was quite unable to make any sense of most of what was said. This does not represent a failure on my part to understand most philosophers (see my correspondence with H.H. Price and C.D.Broad in the appendix). But as a psychiatrist I was familiar with the peculiar flavor of this form of thought disorder. In this, someone may say something, the meaning of which is not actually contained in what is said. The meaning somehow lies behind the stated word, and can never be reached, for each statement made to clarify the first statement also carries its own hidden meaning in turn behind it, and so on. It is like the peels of an infinite onion, at the unreachable center of which, I suspect, lies a fearful emptiness. The meanings in Wittgenstein's philosophy, especially in his later work, follow the same course and perhaps for the same reason. Thus his later enigmatic 'philosophy' does not have its place in the great tradition of British empirical philosophers like Locke, Berkeley, Hume, Broad, Price, Moore, Russell and Ayer who try and clarify matters. But Wittgenstein, after all, was a German-speaking philosopher steeped in the great Teutonic tradition of making things as obscure as possible. Teutonic philosophers like to discuss at great length such topics as the Nature of the Ultimate Essence of Being, or some such. The Teutonic and Anglo-Saxon traditions cannot mix any more than can oil and water. Unfortunately the British intelligentsia have a weak spot for colorful eccentrics from central Europe (usually Vienna), such as satirized by Evelyn Waugh in the person of Otto Silenus in *Decline and Fall*. So, whatever Wittgenstein himself may have suffered from, what went on in these seminars I attended in Cambridge was in my opinion conducted in schizophrenese—or if it was not actually schizophrenese I suggest that the sessions were conducted in a new language which I had never learned. The good English of Locke, Berkeley and Hume, which is the same as that of Russell, Moore and Ayer, can be expanded by introducing new terms to express new ideas, but, whatever its permutations, the language of philosophy must remain good, comprehensible English.

It is no denigration of Wittgenstein to point out a possible clinical cause for the peculiarities of his style and content. Creative people with this type of syndrome are much to be admired for their achievements in the face of adversity. But the creation should not be mistaken for the obstacles that opposed it. It is no insult to be called a (good) poet rather than a (poor) philosopher. Anyone who thinks that Wittgenstein was really a philosopher should read Ayer's *Wittgenstein* and Jenny Teichman's *Philosophy and the Mind*. Ayer struggles for three hundred pages to try and find some meaning in Wittgenstein's writings but at the end he is forced to admit defeat. Philosophy should tell us about the world and how we come to know the world. Wittgenstein does not do this but offers instead an idiosyncratic way of looking at the world—which is poetry.

In some comments some years ago in the London Times, my critics suggested that I might be over-doing the clinical diagnosis of paranoia with regard to people long dead and whose teachings I dislike. I am therefore pleased to quote support from Rescher (1990) who states that:

> " Postmodernistic psychology, philosophy and art (e.g. followers of Freud, Marx, Nietzsche, Russell, Bridgman) are consumed with paranoia and commit *trahison des clercs*...a betrayal by the intellectual *avant-garde* of the fundamental values of communication and community on which alone civilized life can be predicated...but the postmodernists have mercifully got the big picture badly wrong[18]."

Wittgenstein, like Sir Isaac Newton, was also not a very pleasant person, both arrogant and intolerant of the views of others. His style of debate was to steamroller any hint of opposition to his views. He surrounded himself, as people of this stamp commonly do, with a little band of devoted acolytes, including my cousin Yorick Smythies. It cannot be said that my cousin benefited from this relationship. Wittgenstein would discourage his disciples from taking up a career in philosophy, since he, Wittgenstein, had solved all the outstanding problems in that subject. Freddie Ayer told me that everyone in the world of philosophy at Cambridge was terrified of him except Broad, who had a very tough character and who, as always, 'went his own way'.

Another highly negative view of Wittgenstein has been published by John C. Marshall, the Oxford neuropsychologist (1991). His diagnosis is not madness but badness:

> "To this very day, the acolytes of north Oxford preach that current cognitive psychology, artificial intelligence and neuroscience are all based on an awful mistake: the purported failure to realize that language games, not empirical (and theoretical) enquiry, explicate the mental...His mental cramp had ossified to such an extent he could not see that his approach to psychology was strictly analogous to arguing that astronomy should be bounded by analysis of the sentence 'The Sun rises in the East and sets in the West.'."

Marshall asks further whether Wittgenstein intentionally chose students in a strange land who would be incapable of understanding who he was and what he taught. None of this prevents many contemporary philosophers from claiming that Wittgenstein was the 'greatest philosopher of the century'. As far as I can see Wittgenstein's two main intelligible doctrines were that it is impossible to have a private language and that we have do not have any private experiences. However, many children do develop private languages and it is simply false to say we do not have private experiences. Wittgenstein belongs to the romantic poetic tradition of Nietzsche and Sartre rather than the Apollonian philosophical tradition of Berkeley, Locke and Hume

Racism, Sexism and Elitism

A prominent feature of the intelligentsia in some climes today is the epidemic of various forms of vicarious righteous indignation. Many busybodies, instead of concentrating on improving their own characters, work themselves into a lather of righteous indignation over the sins of others. These 'sins' today are not those that drove the Puritans into their own frenzies of self-righteousness. Today's sins are largely confined, by accidents of history, to 'racism', 'sexism' and 'elitism'. In all these three, conceptual confusion reigns.

(i) In 'anti-racism', as a socio-political movement, the confusion is between the concept of 'race' and the concept of 'culture'. It is of course wholly wrong to discriminate against people, to regard them with contempt, to deny their civil rights, because of their skin colour, or their national or racial origin. Unfortunately racism is natural to primitive humans since members of other tribes, no matter how defined, are likely to be enemies to be exterminated rather than otherwise. Much education is required to eliminate 'racist' instincts and even then, as recent events demonstrate all too clearly, the conversion is likely to be skin deep when push comes to shove. A multi-racial society is a worthy goal to aim for. But a multi-cultural society is something else. People from another culture, who emigrate to your country and yet wish to retain their culture encapsulated within your culture, will cause problems[19]. Here I am talking about culture in the anthropological sense and not in the artistic sense. If the two cultures do not conflict over essential items then the merger can be made. But different cultures are likely to differ over such items as value systems, customs, laws, things to admire and things to deplore, etc.[20]. History shows that, if two such incompatible cultures attempt to occupy the same territory, attempt to form one nation or country, then the immigrants must abandon their own culture and assimilate into the host culture. Millions of Jews, Huguenots, Poles, Irish, Hindus, Chinese, West Indians, etc. have come to Britain and America over the last centuries and have settled in quite peaceably enormously enriching the host country. But the results of trying to merge two incompatible cultures are all too evident today in Bosnia, Kosovo, Israel-Palestine, Northern Ireland, and elsewhere.

In particular, a culture, such as Militant Islam, that does not separate matters of state from matters of the religion that defines the culture, is usually unable to compromise on these matters. When the Japanese try to keep non-Japanese out of their country they are denounced as racist. Whereas they are really concerned not with 'race' but with keeping out alien cultures. The immigration of a large number of fundamentalist Islamic Japanese would be far more of a threat to the tranquility of Japan than would the immigration of an equal number of non-Japanese people who did not belong to such a fundamentalist religion and who would therefore, over time, be able to assimilate into Japanese culture. Fundamentalist Christians do not pose this problem because, unlike Fundamentalist Moslems, they recognise the difference between the State and their religion. But to people like the Iranian clerics and to the Taliban regime in Afghanistan the religion is the State.

Every culture has the right, and indeed the duty to its citizens, to keep its own culture more or less intact, and not run the risk of severe domestic turmoil in the future by allowing the mass immigration of members of an incompatible and immutable culture. Again I must emphasize that I am talking about 'culture' in the anthropological, and not the artistic, sense. In art, as in cookery, it is advantageous to encourage a mixture of different cultures as instanced by the effect of African art on painters such as Modigliani and Chinese art on Matisse.

Unfortunately, in some countries, for historical reasons, members of incompatible cultures are already present trying to share the same land. The conflicts in Israel-Palestine, Northern Ireland, Bosnia, Kosovo, much of the former Soviet Union, Somalia, Iraq, etc. are not primarily about race. The Bosnian Moslems are racially very close to the Bosnian Croats and Serbs. Jews and Arabs both belong to the Semitic 'race'. The conflict is between cultures or 'tribes' aggravated by history. What counts is the network and nuances of habits, customs, loyalties, beliefs, values, language, etc. that make up a culture and that define a tribe. Even the minor cultural differences between the French Canadians in Quebec and their Anglophone compatriots threaten enormous difficulties. People who settle in your country and maintain their own culture are not immigrants—they are colonists. For example, some Islamic Kashmiri schoolchildren in a school in England cheered when told of the attack on the World Trade Center are a case in point (see The Daily Telegraph September 15th). There is evidence that Islamic fundamentalists are targeting such children in Britain to obtain recruits for their killing squads. These Islamic Kashmiri groups in Britain shun all contact with mainstream British life and relate only with each other and with their kinfolk in Kashmir. A recent survey of young British born Muslims in Britain revealed that the majority supported Bin Laden and many of them intended to go to Afghanistan to fight for him. Such colonialism has no place in the 21st century.

As Machiavelli records in *The Discourses*, the Romans knew very well that, in order to build an empire, you had either to treat the defeated very well and allow them to keep their own cultures, or you had to destroy the culture completely and enslave the inhabitants. Anything in between leads ultimately only to disaster. We live in a world just recovering from an orgy of empire-building that lasted for centuries, with stronger cultures constantly invading and having to deal after that with the subjugated weaker cultures. The strategy used by the Romans is still true today. Countries where the native culture was effectively destroyed (such as the United States and Australia) today are stable. Countries in which the invaded were treated badly but never destroyed (such as Serbia and Ulster) are unstable. Countries that were invaded but the inhabitants were treated (relatively) well (such as India and New Zealand) are stable. Countries in which two cultures are competing for the same turf vacated by a collapsing empire (such as Palestine in the old Ottoman Empire) will be unstable.

So the critics of 'racism' need to consider in each case whether they are really talking about racism (as in South Africa between blacks and whites) or about a culture clash (as in the former Yugoslavia between three cultures—Catholic, Orthodox and Muslim—and in South Africa between Zulus and the other blacks).

(ii) The entry of a large number of women into business and the professions in Britain and America has led to a spirited attempt to get rid of the male chauvinist customs so deeply engrained in many aspects of our culture. But good things can be taken too far, and in some parts of the US, where good things often *are* taken too far, some feminist fanatics have started a crusade to bring the female sub-culture into conflict at every possible point with the male sub-culture. This is based on a denial that there are not any, or should not be any, inherent psychological differences between men and women, only biological ones. The result has been unpleasant for all concerned. The error lies in turning what should be a matter of concern to individuals into an occasion for a cultural clash and a deep wallow in satisfying tubs of righteous indignation.

(iii) The egalitarian principles that we live by today have a good side and a bad side. The good is the reduction of the excessive privilege and conceit of the rich and the aristocracy. The bad is the curious idea that infects many of the left-wing intelligentsia today, especially in the world of education, that to be in any way better or more talented than others is wicked. So gifted children should not have any special treatment, but should remain bored under-achievers in a class geared to the pace of its dullest members. In addition, the even more curious idea has taken root that there is no such thing as talent anyway. Mozart, on this theory, is no better than Andrew Lloyd Weber; Shakespeare than Rod McKuen. If this is supposed to be a way of reducing envy in our society, then the cure is worse than the disease. Any individual is entitled to say, "I prefer pop music to Mozart". What is illegitimate is for such a person, or for some philosopher defending this position, to say, "Mozart *is* no better than pop music." and to teach this to impressionable young people. I understand that standards at Oxford have fallen so low that a Professor there actually holds these views and communicates them to his students.

Psychopathology and Ideology

We are entitled to ask the question—why have so many obviously psychopathic intellectuals such as Rousseau, Marx, Nietzsche, Heidegger, Sartre, etc. have had such an enormous influence on the world, both through the corruption of individual minds ravaged by their passionate rhetoric, and through the effects on the lives of countless harmless, ordinary people by their lieutenants, such as Robespierre, Lenin, Stalin, Hitler, Mao and Pol Pot? Of course men of a very similar stamp, such as Caligula, Nero and Domitian, came to the top in Imperial Rome without the help of any ideology. But that merely shows what nature can manage for herself if left without the constraints of a healthy ideology. The answer may be that the negative emotions of fear, hatred, envy, guilt and the lust for revenge are stronger than the positive emotions of love, trust, devotion and compassion. These latter have in the past only been able to hold their own with the support of the powerful ethical system supplied by a supernatural religion. But even the effect of such a religion on the world has depended heavily on negative emotions—for example, the manipulation of the universal fear of death by the priesthood for their own purposes, and the incitement of the faithful to torture, burn and massacre infidels. On the positive side these same religions also provide techniques wherewith to lessen the painful impact of guilt and bereavement.

Johnson (1988) gives a detailed account of the moral and personal shortcomings of a number of leading intellectuals, but he goes on to conclude that no intellectual is to be trusted. In fairness he should have given biographies of those intellectuals whose teaching have actually proved beneficial to mankind. Of course, we are not dealing here with intellectuals in general, but only with those who promote some ideological or moral theory (using ideology in the sense put forward in this book as the best translation we can get for Weltanschauung). The trouble is that there have been several good and true prophets but they have had little political influence given the irrational temper of our times and the fact that the media will always promote the romantic, sensational and deadly over the peaceful and sane. Which intellectuals would one nominate whose effect on the world has been mainly good? John Locke, for one, who was the intellectual force behind the American Constitution. Albert Schweitzer for another. Amongst economists I would nominate Adam Smith and Frederick Hayek; among psychologists, William James, Frederick Myers, John Beloff and Alan Gauld; neurologists, Wilder Penfield, Sir Francis Walshe and Sir John Eccles; psychiatrists, Carl Gustav Jung, Ian Stevenson and Victor Frankl; politicians, Mahatma Ghandi and Nelson Mandela; philosophers, Robert Almeder, H. H. Price, C.D. Broad, John Foster; writers, Arthur Koestler, Alexander Solzhenitsyn, Boris Pasternak and Vaclav Havel.

Johnson did not go on to ask why his villains had the major influence that they did, nor what we should do in future to avoid these terrible mistakes. Distrusting *all* intellectuals is not practical advice. Intellectuals today exert their influence on the masses by their writings rather than by their life styles, with a very few exceptions such as Albert Schweitzer. The effect of the tragi-comic attempts of Bertrand Russell and Sartre to involve themselves in the practical politics of revolt were insignificant compared with the influence of what they wrote. But it seems to be true that what people are determines to a large extent the content of their writings, when they are dealing with such topics as the nature of humanity and giving advice about what people should, or should not, believe in, or do, as moral, political and artistic beings. It is hardly possible, for instance, that the historical Jesus and Prince Gautama were monsters whose historic 'images' as people were skillfully concocted by devoted disciples.

Furthermore, the writings of Rousseau, Marx, Wagner, Nietzsche, Sartre, etc. with all their romantic glamour, eloquence and poetry appeal to the psychopath that lurks in the shadows in many overtly civilized and decent people. How many Germans, for example, would otherwise remained all their lives their 'normal' decent selves, but, demoralized by the injustices of the Versailles treaty, the collapse of the mark and the rigors of the Great Depression, were swept up and away by the hypnotic magic of Hitler's oratory and the soul-stirring theatre of the Nuremberg rallies to give their passionate support to one of the vilest regimes of all time?

What then can we suggest should be done to improve on Johnson's recommendations? I suggest that we need to strike right at the heart of the matter. This entire revolt against morals, decency and reason derives its origins and authority over the twentieth century mind from the underlying doctrine that people are soulless automata, a doctrine backed, so we are told, by the overwhelming prestige of modern science. However, the actual facts and theories of neuroscience do not lead to any such conclusion, which is actually based on metaphysical and quasi-religious speculations of the mind-brain Identity Theorists. The Identity Theory states that the mind and the brain are the same and denies that we have souls. In fact modern neuroscience and introspection psychology are actually quite incompatible with the Identity Theory. An uncritical belief in the Identity Theory is no longer good enough as I have argued elsewhere (Smythies, 1994b). Moreover Identity Theorists studiously ignore the data from parapsychology, which to any unbiased observer, present a strong case that this whole matter needs rethinking. Julian Huxley (1957), for one, stated that there is a good *prima facie* case for the existence of telepathy and clairvoyance. What parapsychology has lacked up to now is any theory that can account for its findings within the framework of a general scientific theory of the world; and this, Cartesian Dualism and the Identity Theory both fail to do. But now such a theory—the Theory of Extension—has been provided (Smythies, 1994a) within an expanded and unitary physics (see Chapter 3). It would obviously be much healthier for people to realize that the question of the immortal human soul is still an open scientific question, as Walshe (1953) and Robert Almeder (1992) have argued eloquently, and not one prematurely closed by bad metaphysics masquerading as science.

The rise of Scientific Materialism

The Romantic Revival culminated in the Wagnerian fantasies of the Third Reich. Since then it has been replaced by the attempt to apply various scientific developments, usually out of context and tainted with reductionism, to practical human affairs. These include current theories in psychology and philosophy, psychoanalysis and psychotherapy, Marxism, evolution and ideas derived from artificial intelligence (AI) to a consideration of which I will now return.

A very important factor in the decay of Western Civilization over the last century has been the gradual but relentless shift in the dominant cultural belief in the nature of humanity that took root in intellectual circles at this time and from there seeped down over the decades to color and then dominate 'common sense'—the thoughts and beliefs of the common folk. This involved the shift away from the view of a person with an immortal destiny as the creation of a loving and concerned Supernatural Being, to the view that a person is nothing but a biochemical eddy in a closed, wholly impersonal universe, of no greater importance than a wave beating on a beach or an swirl of dust in the desert wind—with no immortal destiny or indeed any other kind of destiny other than what the laws of physics and chemistry ordain for the fate of his physical body, and what the laws of sociology and psychology ordain for his social fate—just a collection of atoms hurrying soundlessly, meaninglessly into a biophysical future. The orthodox doctrine of contemporary science is that human beings are nothing more than soulless biochemical mechanisms totally immersed in a deterministic universe.

If the modern orthodox scientific account is true then, of course, most religions, including Christianity, Hinduism and Islam are false, since most are based in different ways on the concept that the essential core of the human personality survives the death of the physical body. If most religions are false then, as Nietzsche so passionately proclaimed, the clergy must have been peddling delusions over the centuries and the Judeo-Christian basis of Western Civilization should be replaced by something else. But what? The attempt to return to the world of the Herrenvolk, that is German tribalism, came to nothing except the murder of millions of people in concentration camps, war and the Holocaust. The attempt to establish the atheistic religion of Communism has also come to nothing except the murder of another thirty million or so people, and the ruination of the people, their psychology and economy, of one sixth of the world.

Cognitive science today is dominated by an amalgam of the mind-brain Identity Theory and scientific materialism. Critics have complained that this has resulted in a body of inflexible dogma, and an inability to consider alternative views.

Brian Pippard says (1992):

> "There are those however, who have gone further and assumed authority in the name of science, to brand all belief as superstition. They have abandoned healthy skepticism in favor of bigotry...But, whatever individual scientists may say, it is not true that science has cut away the roots of revealed religion. This is beyond its power, though its legitimate techniques have starved the roots of material nourishment and thus weakened or destroyed the faith of the merely credulous."[21].

Any wholly biological theory of people suffers from the moral disadvantage that it offers us no rational defense against the doctrines of Adolf Hitler. In biological Darwinism it is simply the survival of the species that counts. In social Darwinism it is only the survival of the tribe that counts. Hitler proclaimed that the Germans were a Master Race. He failed in his political aims, but what would the social Darwinists have said if he had been successful? Suppose Hitler had won the battle of Britain and the battle of Stalingrad—which he very nearly did—had totally conquered Europe and reduced Russia to a cipher, whilst his allies the Japanese had done the same to Asia. Africa could have put up no resistance and the Africans would have provided a useful source of slaves. The United States would have been completely isolated and at Hitler's mercy (by his control of the oil fields of the Middle East).

Then there could be no biological argument against the claim that the Germans really were the Master Race for their half of the world and the Japanese of their half. These two races would have done all that evolution had required of them. Their selfish genes would have flourished and the selfish genes of their rival races (Slavs, Jews, Arabs, Negroes, Indians, Chinese, etc.) would have withered. In biological terms the Germans are not a Master Race only because Hitler lost these key battles. Since consistent eliminative materialists lump the concept of humanist values with despised folk psychology, they could not, without being inconsistent, have greeted Hitler's triumph with anything but (biological) approval. Who mourns today for Neanderthal man? The reaction that the Nazi regime was monstrous is based on our humanist tradition, which in turn is based on the teachings of individual people like Socrates and the Buddha as well as the Essenes. The humanist values we revere today certainly did not come from Classical Rome. Militant Islam is flourishing but it remains a threat to, not a supporter of, Western civilization, as it has been for over a thousand years.

Even the arch materialist Gilbert Ryle (1924) had some other feelings about the matter:

> "...I hate cynicism and though I have not in the ordinary sense of the words *a* religion or *a* faith, yet I understand what the former is and I know that the latter is something which holds life together and makes it true and is not itself a mere collection of accepted dogmas and beliefs but is the real thing in life that is not just surface."

In view of the painful character of much of human life in an unfriendly and apparently badly constructed universe, it is certainly easier to maintain an optimistic ethic and emotional peace of mind, (if only to keep despair at bay with no ambition for Augustan tranquility) if one believes that people have, or could have, some kind of existence after the death, decay and corruption of their physical bodies. How often have we read the words in obituaries and biographies "She was sustained in the midst of all her sorrows by her steadfast religious faith"? How just it would be if all the unfairness and tragedy of this life were compensated for by events in some future life, as taught by the Hindu doctrine of Karma and by Christian and Moslem beliefs. But, of course, whether or not this happens is purely a matter of fact, and we should certainly not base our opinions on ancient myths, faulty arguments and wishful thinking. But equally we should not reject the possibility on the basis of meek acceptance of allegedly scientific dogma based on a decrepit metaphysics. The branch of science that attempts to look directly into this question is psychical research, also called parapsychology. This has not yet come up with any firm answers one way or the other but is certainly a direction in which we should keep looking (Almeder 1992, Heywood, 1961, Huxley 1957). It seems sadly true that someone, who denies his or her own immortal destiny, and even more so a society that has given up its belief in the immortal destiny of its members, is likely to fall prey to systems of belief promulgating the immortal destiny of something else—the Third Reich or the Communist Party for example.

The great advances in the biological sciences over the last century have led in many people's opinion to a progressive strengthening of the Identity Theory of mind-brain relationships. Many neuroscientists and neurophilosophers, whom I have met, froth at the mouth at the mildest suggestion that this theory could even *possibly* be wrong; well, not actually froth but nevertheless instantly don a sardonic mask of surprise at the very idea that anyone could be so naïve and (almost) politically incorrect even to think such an heretical thought. Unfortunately, people living in a culture that accepted this theory as *true*, are all too easily led from the statement that people *are* mere physico-chemical machines, to the idea that people should be treated *as* mere physico-chemical machines, as did the late East German government that prided itself on its scientific credentials, for example.

There are two ideologies that lead to atrocities. The first is that the next world is all important, and that our religion has the only key to entry; thus we are only doing Christian heretics a favor in the long run when we burn them at the stake in order to save their souls, or if we execute infidels on the spot if they do not convert to Islam. The second is the belief that this world is the only world there is and so nothing we do here will ever attract punishment in any non-existent world to come. So there is absolutely nothing to stop us putting undesirable people into gas chambers or in the Gulag, if we think this will be good for us, or for the race, or for the party. If human biology is all there is, and all folk psychology is so much garbage, then all ideas that come from this folk psychology, such as truth, beauty, altruism and decency must be replaced by the socio-biological ideas of social Darwinism. You cannot have it both ways. Of course, atrocities often happen on the basis of the very primitive ideology of tribalism, as a by-product of tribal wars over territory, slavery and genocide. It is surely a telling indictment of the Scientific Age in which we live that it coincides with, and I would say does nothing to prevent, the present epidemic of tribal warfare (embellished by the latest advances in the technology of germ and neurotoxin warfare) and genocide (or 'ethnic cleansing' in the "Newspeak" of our times) on a scale that no mere primitive tribe ever attained.

The only ideological system under which people are likely ever to live peaceably together is one in which scientists stop preaching that they *know* that people are nothing but biochemical machines; in which religious leaders cease claiming that *their* system contains the only road to truth and salvation; and in which the culture can provide a centripetal force stronger that the centrifugal forces of tribalism that today are tearing so much of the world apart. I suggest that one of the main causes of the deterioration of all aspects of our culture today is the official doctrine of contemporary science that people are things.

How could a mere four hundred years of science, conducted by such puny intellects on so insignificant a planet have led to such arrogance?

One would hope that scientists should be more sensitive to the likely psychological and social consequences of their professional activity when they leave their own specialist fields and launch out into the uncharted surrounding wastes of metaphysics. As Stent (1987) says in his review in *Science* of Patricia Smith Churchland's *Neurophilosophy* :

> "Where neuroscientists and psychologists do need philosophical help is in fathoming not the physical but the metaphysical infrastructure of folk presuppositions and myths and the likely consequences of their abandonment. Churchland is not one of the folks who can provide that help."

Stent supports Kant's hypothesis that we live in two metaphysically distinct worlds. There is the scientific one in which natural objects, including brains, are governed by the laws of causal determination. The second is the world of the practical reason of ethics where a person's actions are governed by the laws of freedom that individual free will imposes. His concept of free will is based on the "...logically necessary constituents of the individualistic theory of personhood that governs interpersonal human relations". Page (1957) puts it even more urgently "But without the guiding mind, the brain comes to little. This is not a problem to be approached lightly, for the worlds of belief, faith, of beauty, and of happiness are at stake".

Scientists today are going through a period of feeling that almost everything fundamental about the universe and its contents has been discovered and all that remains is filling in a mass of details— an attitude that also prevailed at the end of the last century. This belief leads to intolerance toward those bold or rash enough to disagree with the orthodoxy. In contrast, some leading physicists, such as Roger Penrose (1989) and Andrei Linde (1990), claim that current physics by no means presents a nearly complete picture of the natural world, and that there may yet be revolutionary developments in store on a level with relativity and quantum theory. There is still much to be explored in the world, the nature of phenomenal consciousness and whether higher-dimensional space has any contents, for example.

An example of this form of arrogant dogmatism that disfigures much of contemporary science is contained in what contributors to the journal *Nature* have to say, from time to time, about parapsychology. The scorn and derision to which many pioneers like Semmelweiss and Pasteur were subjected to by their fellow scientists is today being visited on practitioners of the infant science of parapsychology[22]. The critics know *a priori* that phenomena such as telepathy are impossible; so no amount of evidence will ever convince them, just as the Churchmen of the 17th century refused to look through Galileo's telescope because they knew *a priori* that Jupiter has no moons. Contrary to present superstition, science has not demonstrated in any way that the experimentally based claims of parapsychologists are false. What has really happened is that many scientists have adopted *a priori* a particular metaphysical theory (the Identity Theory) of mind-brain relations that, if true, would render such phenomena as telepathy impossible. But it is highly unlikely that the Identity Theory is a tenable *scientific* theory (Smythies, 1994 a, b) so we can no longer adhere to this verdict on parapsychology.

Most scientists specialize very early. The competitive pressures are immense, and to stay ahead the young scientist has perforce to concentrate on the sciences basic to his craft and on the theories and techniques in his own tiny area. There is no time to gain a broader platform for one's scientific beliefs and to attain the expertise that will enable one to distinguish between scientific theory and metaphysical speculation disguised as scientific theory. So a prominent neuroscientist may know very little about other branches of science—introspectionist psychology, clinical neuropsychiatry, or cosmology, for example—and still less about epistemology, ontology and the philosophy of perception and of mind-brain relations. One eminent neuroscientist (Mountcastle, 1985) assured me that there was no mind-brain problem to worry about. He has since stated publicly "Dualism is dead: thank goodness". His argument is that his experiments and those of his colleagues in the neurosciences will produce a definitive body of knowledge about how the brain works. This knowledge, accumulated steadily over the years, would *by itself* increase the probability that the Identity Theory is true, until such a time as this probability would be close enough to so as to convince even the most hardened skeptic. The bold theories and high technical expertise exhibited in modern neuroscience unfortunately gives rise in these scientists to an attitude that other people, whose opinions are not based on their own technical expertise in this area, are not to be taken seriously. Thus they fail even to listen to any criticism from the despised 'philosophers'. Such is the road to hubris.

This attitude reveals a complete inability to grasp the essential nature of the problem involved. As Bertrand Russell (1948) and Ayer (1952) pointed out many years ago, if we have one set of events a and a second set of events b, and if we want to demonstrate that $a=b$, then it is pointless to rely simply on piling up information about a, or for that matter about b. We have to demonstrate that in fact a and b are identical. As Ayer (1952) put it so clearly:

> "If this [the mind-brain relation] is a genuine problem, it is hard to see why further information about the brain should be expected to solve it...For however much we amplify our picture of the brain, it remains still a picture of something physical, and it is just the question how anything physical can interact with something that is not that is supposed to constitute our difficulty. If what we are seeking is a bridge across a seemingly impassable river it will not help us merely to elevate one of its banks."

The actual mind-brain problem may be expressed "What is the relation between our sensations (and related images), information about which we obtain by introspection, and their correlated brain events, information about which we gain by exteroception (perception)?" A theory designed to answer *this* question cannot be expressed in terms of brain mechanisms alone. Both statements about the phenomenology of our sensations (S) (and images) and statements about brain mechanisms (B) must logically enter into the formulations of the theory, even if the theory is as simple as S equals B or S does not equal B. Of course, evidence about how the brain works may be *relevant* to competing hypotheses in this field but this evidence by itself cannot *establish* such an hypothesis, contrary to Mountcastle's belief. In fact, the current scientific evidence is incompatible with the Identity hypothesis. It would still be a valid question even if we knew every detail, in biochemical, biophysical and cybernetic terms, of how every neuron and synapse in the brain works, both singly and in combination. The data obtained by introspectionist psychologists represents basic data about the universe and cannot be reduced to, nor contradicted by any neurophysiological theory. For example, if I observe, during an experiment on after-images, that this clear-cut after-image that I am currently observing is clearly red and clearly round, then no theorist will ever persuade me that it is really yellow and square. Thus, in any mature science of the mind and brain, sensations, and their observable properties, and neurons and their observable properties, must both be mentioned. Otherwise the theory may be a theory about the brain, but it is not a theory about the relationship between the brain and mental entities (particulars) such as sensations and images. It can certainly be a theory about the relation between mental *functions,* such as intelligence or memory, and brain events, but not mental *entities*.

Most neuroscientists, because of their over-specialization, are ignorant of these elementary points of logic. If one mentions to many young neuroscientists the name of Sir John

Eccles, perhaps the most prominent dualist in neurophysiology in recent times, they have a tendency to shake their heads and to imply what a pity it is that a scientist brilliant enough to win a Nobel Prize should succumb to ancient superstitions and advocate a dualist theory of mind. Such an attitude is based entirely on the enormous gaps in their own education, on their own over-simplification of a complex problem, on the fact that they do not understand the issues involved, and on a preference for basing the opinions and judgment in this field on dogma rather than rational argument. They all take a highly dubious metaphysical theory—the Identity Theory—as some kind of established scientific gospel with a most unfortunate effect on the validity of their arguments. Neuroscientists who pronounce on philosophical and metaphysical matters, and few seem to be able to resist the temptation to do so—once they become sufficiently eminent—should at least have studied widely and deeply in these fields and preferably have taken formal professional training in at least the key aspects of them (as I did in philosophy with Avrum Stroll many years ago). Otherwise they are likely, in all innocence, to make the most obvious mistakes in logic, and to fall into all kind of traps with which these fields are strewn for the unwary (see Smythies, 1994a,b)[23].

There was a Door to which I found no Key:
There was a Veil past which I could not see:
Some little Talk awhile of ME and THEE
There seemed—and then no more of THEE and ME.

Omar Khayyám

CHAPTER 3.

The identification of mind and brain: a maelstrom of error and confusion.

Almost all neuroscientists, including cognitive scientists and psychologists, today adhere firmly to the belief that the theory of psychoneural identity has been established as a true scientific hypothesis on a level with relativity and Darwinian evolution. An enormous amount of information has been gathered over the course of the last one hundred years, at an ever-increasing rate, about the functional anatomy and neurochemistry of the brain, and the role of its various mechanisms in perception, ideation, emotion, and action at a number of different levels (anatomy, physiology, biochemistry, biophysics, computational cybernetics) of the reductionist hierarchy. All this evidence is held to support the Identity Hypothesis. However, there is, in fact, not one atom of evidence from neuroscience, or anywhere else, to support the philosophical theory of mind-brain identity[24].

Its adherents claim that the mind-brain Identity Hypothesis is supported by the following arguments:—

(1) The mind is just a folk name for certain of the operations of the brain, with which it is identical. When a neuroscientist studies the brain she finds only a vast number of nerve cells connected to each other by nerve nets of unfathomable complexity. They function, as far as she can tell, as purely biophysical machines using information processing techniques, such as parallel distributed processing, familiar to designers of

computers and other information-processing and distributing machines. She does not find any trace of any dualistic 'mind' interacting with this system (but then she had never looked for any).

(2) The evidence from neuropsychiatry and neurology shows that in cases of severe brain degeneration, such as Alzheimer's disease, the patient will eventually lose all mental capacities and be reduced to a purely vegetable existence. This too is held as certain evidence that mind and brain are identical.

(3) The evidence from artificial intelligence (AI) is held to prove that there can be, neither logically nor empirically, any essential difference between a human mind and an advanced computer of sufficient power and complexity particularly one using parallel distributed processing rather than linear techniques. Alan Turing claimed to have demonstrated this by his test, which says that if a computer and a person cannot be distinguished by their responses to any sufficiently extensive range of questions, then the principles by which the operate must be the same.

(4) It is maintained that the alternative dualist theory associated with the name of Descartes, in which the mind is held to be something different from the brain and that the two interact, has by now been refuted, both empirically by the advances in cognitive neuroscience and by logical analysis, so that it is no longer a serious contender. Descartes claimed that the brain is an extended physical object and that the mind is an unextended, thinking spirit. Neuroscientists, and most philosophers, no longer believe in thinking spirits.

This account of the nature of mind is currently not only the orthodox theory of science but also of most philosophers and furthermore, after a hundred years of downward percolation, it is the view taken by the intelligentsia in general. However, it is not yet the view of the general population: surveys taken in the United States show that most people still believe in the existence of an after-life of some kind[24].

I will examine the scientific and philosophical logic of these arguments in order.

Argument (1). The brain is certainly only a physico-chemical machine; but it is still entirely an open question whether it is a machine developed to *generate* consciousness or a machine that *liaises* with consciousness, just as William James phrased it a century ago, or as Hippocrates put it "The brain is the messenger to the mind". Eccles (1953) has suggested that this liaison is conducted by minute 'mind influences'. The techniques of neuroscience and physics have never detected any such postulated 'mind influences' but then none of these techniques was ever designed to do so. The neuroscientist *starts* his researches into the function of the brain with the simplifying assumption, which is perfectly valid for this purpose, that the brain is a physico-chemical machine functioning according to the laws of chemistry and contemporary physics. But he cannot claim at the end of the day that he has discovered that the brain is a machine that generates rather than liaises with mind. For he has only discovered the assumption that he started out with. The footsteps he has found in the sand are his own. If the mind interacts with its brain by causal interactions of a subtle kind, then the present techniques of neurophysiology could not detect them. Techniques specifically designed to do this are required. I have suggested elsewhere in outline how this might be done (Smythies, 1994a).

Argument (2). The argument from neuropsychiatry relating to conditions like Alzheimer's disease only shows that certain brain events are *necessary* for ordinary mental events to occur. It does not show that they are *necessary and sufficient* for the mental events to occur. Whatever the brain is, it is certainly a computerised representative or signaling mechanism. Representative mechanisms come in two varieties: those in which the output is coded (examples are the telegraph and the semaphore), and those in which the output is uncoded (examples are the cinema and television). Our visual mechanisms belong to the second class, since the visual field in consciousness bears an uncoded but topographically organized representation, in the

form of the *visual field*, of that part of the world around us before
our eyes, that forms the *stimulus field* (Smythies, 1996). The visual
field, therefore, *represents* the stimulus field. The intermediate
parts of this mechanism, of course, lying between the retina and
the visual field, deal with information coded in the brain in the
form of the frequency and pattern of timing in axonal spikes and
cortical rhythms. These mechanisms operate by using vectorial
codes involving differential synaptic weighting of synapses in
nerve nets as well as the formation of new synapses and the
pruning of old ones (Smythies, 1997a,b). But the final product of
all this computation is the purely topographically coded visual
field that we experience in consciousness, what Crick (1994)
calls "a vivid internal picture of the external world". Similarly in
television the output is the topographically organized picture
on the TV screen that is uncoded in the ordinary sense. Any
child can understand what the TV set is representing. But
information in the intermediate mechanisms (TV camera,
transmission and receiving systems) is indeed coded. All the
events in the TV system, that take place *prior* to the final raster,
or pixel system, that builds up the TV picture, are *necessary* but
they are not *necessary and sufficient* for television to work. The
TV screen is necessary too. Likewise in the cinema the film
is necessary, but not necessary and sufficient, for the showing
of the movie. The screen is also necessary. Kosslyn (1990) has
very aptly likened after-images to afterglows on the screen of
a cathode ray oscilloscope. However, neuroscience at present
is totally unable to find any structure in the brain that could
mechanically function in this manner i.e. to build up the visual
field that we experience in consciousness in all its spatio-
temporal complexity, in what Francis Crick described as all its
'brilliant technicolour". The appropriate technology to answer
this question comes not from computer technology but from
television technology. We will return to this point later.

Argument (3). According to the Turing-machine argument
from the field of Artificial Intelligence, given a sufficiently
advanced technology, the intelligent responses of a computer
can be made indistinguishable from the intelligent responses of

a human being to a series of questions, so that a person hidden behind a screen would not be able to find out whether he was communicating with the computer or the person. This, the AI theorists claim, means that the computer must have a conscious mind as a person does. A leading AI theorist Marvin Minsky likes to say, "The brain is only a computer made of meat". But this argument depends on a purely behaviourist theory of mind and it does not do justice to the nature of human experience as this is studied by introspectionist psychology. That is, a human being has a direct source of knowledge by introspecting her own sensations, images and thoughts that make up the content of her phenomenal consciousness. Philosophers have tended to take the position either that introspection is infallible ("how could you doubt that you are in pain?") or that it is so unreliable as to be worthless. The answer depends on what it is you are trying to introspect. Experiments have shown that introspection, as a means of determining one's motives for certain actions, is pretty unreliable. Trying to introspect the mind's introspection is equally unrewarding. But introspection, if properly carried out, can give us perfectly reliable scientific data on such matters as the colour of a certain after-image, or whether the blind spot gets filled in when it is positioned over a plaid pattern, or the colour of the visual field when we are in the dark (i.e. black), etc.. In somatic sensation introspection allows an amputee to tell us that when we touch him on the face that he feels the touch on the little finger of his phantom limb rather than on the face (see Ramachandran's studies on these topics).

You can examine your own sensations, both veridical and hallucinatory, as well as your own familiar after-images and can determine for yourself that they possess certain undeniable properties. For example, visual after-images are coloured and have a particular shape. It is difficult to determine the exact shade of colour, or to describe the exact shape. Nevertheless you can be certain that it is a sort of red and not a sort of blue, and that is squareish rather than roundish. It is clearly extended in space and has a boundary that is a Jordan curve i.e. that divides the space of the visual field uniquely into one 'inside' and one 'outside'. This is not a matter of any cognitive judgment on our part, although we can, if we like, make the cognitive judgment 'that after-image is a red one' at any time we choose. The after-image has these properties even when we are not making cognitive judgments about it. These are *intrinsic* properties of the after-image. Similar arguments apply to the nature of our sensations and to other types of images, and to somatic as well as visual sensation. Turing's test fails to address the phenomenal aspects of mind at all and is therefore worthless. Other highly sophisticated objections to the Turing test have been made by Penrose (1989).

Argument (4). The Cartesian Theory of mind has been attacked on several grounds:

(a) It has been held to be logically impossible for things so different as extended and unextended entities to interact.

(b) Even if this were logically possible, it is claimed in practice that it is impossible to understand scientifically, or even imagine, how such different entities could interact.

(c) The theory runs counter to the current dogma that the laws of physics do not allow any such interactions between physical objects such as brains and immaterial thinking spirits.

(d) Neuroscience and evolution currently give a single coherent and intellectually satisfying account of how brains arose during evolution and how they operate by exquisitely engineered operations that scientists feel explain all the 'mental' properties of organisms. They strongly oppose any attempt to graft extraneous 'minds', especially spirits that lie outside this explanatory system, onto this beautiful scientific theory.

We can reply to these objections as follows.

Objection (a): The claim that unextended minds and extended brains cannot, for logical reasons, interact in the way that Descartes suggested has been answered effectively by Richardson (1982). He points out that to ask *how* mind acts on body is an illegitimate question logically equivalent to the question of why light travels in straight lines, or why space is curved. As he says "Gravitational force will be fundamental and to ask how it works will be illegitimate". There is nothing in the logic of causation that says that both partners in a causal relation must be extended. One partner, or indeed both, may well be unextended. Likewise there is nothing in the logic of causation, as Price (1965) has pointed out, that says that events in one space-time system cannot bear causal relations with events in another space-time system. Mijuskovic (1978) supports this contention: "A cause and its effect are different; consequently it is possible for material conditions to have immaterial activities, which in turn refer to and are influenced by physical objects".

Objection (b).

We can deal very quickly with the objection that we cannot even imagine what it would be like for an unextended, immaterial entity to interact with an extended material entity: as the Churchlands have frequently argued in another context, arguments from ignorance are not worth much.

It is certainly true that Cartesian Dualism fails to give any convincing detailed account of how the interaction of an immaterial, thinking spirit with its brain, even if logically and empirically *possible*, in practice yields the phenomena of consciousness as we know them. That which perceives and thinks in us—the Self. 'I' or Pure Ego—seems to itself to lack extension in space. But it interacts, not directly with states of its own brain, nor with external physical objects, but with its own sensations (including the bodily sensations that make up the body-image), images and thoughts. Some of these (visual and somatic sensations and images) have the intrinsic property of extension in space, whereas others of these (the other forms of sensations and images as well as thoughts) lack any such extension. In the Cartesian theory the unextended 'mind' is supposed to react directly with its own physical brain. But it is never explained how this manages to transform the vectorially coded information in the nerve nets of the brain, that represent the external world in this way, into the topographically organized visual field—the picture of the world, as Crick puts it, that we experience so vividly in consciousness. Nor does the Cartesian theory explain in detail, rather than in principle, how the 'will' manages to affect just those millions of neurons out of the billions in the premotor cortex in the precise pattern needed to carry out a complex consciously directed behaviour.

The new rival Theory of Extension or material dualism (that *includes* the Cartesian theory rather than totally replaces it), put very briefly, states that the events that we experience in consciousness—our sensations, images, thoughts and emotions—are located outside the physical world and outside the brain, not in an unextended Cartesian 'spiritual' world, but as organized events in a space of their own—phenomenal space. The connection between the spatio-temporally ordered events in the phenomenal world of consciousness and the spatio-temporally ordered events in the world described by contemporary physics may be *causal* and not one of *identity*. The concept to be grasped is simplicity itself, even if unfamiliar to non-mathematicians. Therefore, to explain consciousness, it may be necessary to revise our most basic concepts of space and time (Smythies, 2003), as I will explain later.

One of the few philosophers to appreciate the key importance of the difference between phenomenal space and time and physical space and time is Thomas Nagel (1993):—

> "Further, for all three of these types of sensation (auditory, visual and tactile), the relations in experiential space and in experiential time among sensory events provide promising targets for analysis. I am talking here about a <u>mental</u> relation, whose connection with physical space and time in the brain remains an open question, one which a psychophysical theory must address...I think it is inevitable that the pursuit of such an account [a unified psychophysical theory] will lead to an alteration of our conception of the physical world...In the long run, therefore, physiological psychology should expect cosmological results. This should not be surprising, since physical science has not heretofore tried to take on consciousness: when it does, the effort will transform it radically."

Objections (c) and (d), These arguments may be countered as follows. Whether independent minds of some kinds exist and interact with brain or not is purely an empirical matter of fact. Either they do or they do not. Logical analysis does not tell us they cannot. And if they do there is no reason at all why they should be Cartesian minds, for there are other criteria of difference between 'minds' and brains besides extension in space, as we will see. Physics up to now has focused entirely on the public physical world and upon causal interactions within that world as a closed system. It has never considered very deeply the nature of the 'observer'. Is the 'observer' described by Einstein in his development of special relativity the same as the 'observer' ('O') described in the course of experiments in introspectionist psychology? Clearly not, for the former is the person of the scientist as a physical object in the physical world being examined, whereas the latter is a phenomenon entirely within consciousness. Nor has physics ever considered the very real possibility that the 'universe' it currently describes may not be a closed system but may be affected by influences coming from outside the four-dimensional space-time continuum. We will see later what 'outside' here could mean. So it would lack any semblance of logic to claim that such 'mind influences' do not exist because no one has ever detected them (no one has ever looked for them!) or because they do not play any role in contemporary physics. Events in the brain must obey the Laws of Nature, but it would be rash to claim that the present laws of physics represent any final statement of the Laws of Nature, as Penrose (1989) has pointed out. For spirited defenses of Cartesian Dualism see John Foster's *The Immaterial Self* and Geoffrey Madell's *Mind and Materialism*.

To return to the main argument: all theories seeking to reduce psychology to physics suffer from the following fatal defect. Modern physics can give no explanation of our conscious sense of the passage of time, or indeed of the passage of time itself. This, as Comfort (1989) has pointed out, has a "devastating effect" on dynamic theories such as Darwinian evolution, which is based on Newtonian physics and cosmology.

These deal with three-dimensional spatial objects moving about in one-dimensional time. In the orthodox Minkowski interpretation of special relativity there are no such objects. They are replaced by the world lines of 'objects' in a block universe in four-dimensional space-time. As Louis de Broglie (1959) put it

"Each observer, as his time passes, discovers, so to speak, new slices of space-time which appear to him as successive aspects of the material world, though in reality the ensemble of events constituting space-time exist prior to his knowledge of them...the aggregate of past, present and future phenomena are in some sense given *a priori*."

The Professor of Physics at the Open University Russell Stannard (1987) gives the same account

"Physics itself recognizes no special moment called 'now'—the moment that acts as the focus for the process of 'becoming' and divides the 'past' from the 'future'. In four-dimensional space-time nothing changes, there is no flow of time, everything simply *is*...It is only in consciousness that we come across the particular time known as 'now'...It is only in the context of mental time that it makes sense to say that all of physical space-time *is*. One might even go so far as to say that it is unfortunate that such dissimilar entities as physical time and mental time should carry the same name!"

The Professor of Mathematics at the University of Oxford Roger Penrose (1994) says that in the universe described by special relativity "...particles do not even move, being represented by 'static' curves drawn in space-time." If particles do not even move, then organisms do not move either. According to this theory (the Minkowski interpretation of special relativity) what we perceive as moving organisms are really successive cross-sections of their immobile four-dimensional world lines to which the Newtonian *dynamic* concepts of Darwinian theory cannot apply. What Darwinian theory describes are really *structural* features of space-time which are different when located in the 'past' as compared with the 'future'. Organisms only struggle for survival in a Newtonian world. In the world of Special Relativity the appearance of struggle—what *we* perceive as a struggle—is extracted from the particular four-dimensional structure of the world lines of the organisms and projected by the televisual mechanisms of perception as moving three-dimensional images in a visual field in a human consciousness.

Einstein (1961) himself saw this point clearly:

"Since there exist in this four dimensional structure no longer any sections which represent "now" objectively, the concepts of happening and becoming are indeed not completely suspended, but yet complicated. It appears therefore more natural to think of physical reality as a four dimensional existence, instead of, as hitherto, the *evolution* of a three dimensional existence."

As Hughlings Jackson wrote "The doctrine of evolution has nothing to do with the nature of the relationship of psychical to physical states on the highest nervous centres: it simply affirms concomitance of psychical states with states of these centres" (quoted by Walshe, 1953). Markosian (1992) adds "The point of this paper has been to show that those who wish to debate the question of whether time passes cannot settle the debate merely by discussing linguistic matters." The theory of evolution is certainly true: it is just that it needs to be stated differently. If Special Relativity is correct, then Darwin's theory is really concerned with complex differences in the static 4D structure of organisms in different locations in space-time, and not with the evolution of changes in their 3D structure and movement during the course of an independent time.

Thus modern physics and Darwinian theory, in its present form, fail to give any account of one key function of the mind—our sense of the passage of time—i.e. that it is 2006 when I *now* write these words. All physicists agree that in the block universe of special relativity there is no *now*. This in itself proves that it is impossible to reduce consciousness (in which time passes) to physics (in which it doesn't). Penrose and Davies are reduced to calling the subjective sense of the passage of time an "illusion". But there is nothing illusory in the fact that I am writing these words in the year 2006. The solution to this paradox may be that the 'now' of time and its passage are functions of the independent mind and the site and nature of its interaction with its brain. This concept was first put forward in 1906 by the remarkable mathematician C. H. Hinton :— "Passing to four dimensions and our space, we can conceive that all things and movements in our world are the reading off of a permanent reality by a space of consciousness."[25] I discuss this important point more fully in *The Walls of Plato's Cave*. However, even if we accept the Newtonian version of the theory of evolution, there is no reason why a brain that is the outcome of dynamic evolutionary processes should not also be a device able to detect or be influenced by Eccles's minute mind influences.

I do not accept Cartesian Dualism on the grounds that it uses the wrong criterion—extension in space—to distinguish between minds and brains. This criterion actually and primarily is a distinction within phenomenal consciousness itself, as we have seen. As Lord Brain (1955) said

> "...it is essential to recognise the distinction between the space of perception and the space of physics, and between physical objects and perceptual objects—a point stressed in recent years by a number of writers (Köhler, 1938; Russell, 1948; Hutton, 1950; Brain, 1951; Smythies, 1954). It is especially important when speaking of the body or the brain to make it clear whether it is the perceptual or the physical body or brain to which reference is being made."

I also hold the argument 4 (b) above (that Cartesian dualism fails to give any convincing account of how the unextended mind interacts with its brain) is valid, whereas the others are not. I follow Walshe (1951, 1953) in his eloquent claim against the argument that modern science has proven beyond all reasonable doubt that the traditional concept of the soul is untrue and I agree with his statement that the whole argument is in fact metaphysics masquerading as science.

If we attempt to relate mind to brain it is essential to start with the correct theory of mind. And for this purpose the concepts provided by introspectionist psychology are better than those provided by Gilbert Ryle's dispositional theory of mind, or those by philosophers interested in such concepts as 'subjectivity' or 'intentionality', in which terms much of the debate has hitherto been conducted. Introspectionist psychology deals with a number of events that we can observe in our own consciousness. The list of these phenomena is simple and short. We can observe visual, auditory, somatic, gustatory and olfactory sensations and images. There are also pains and emotions that are specialized types of somatic sensations. Lastly there are non-imaged thoughts. Introspectionist psychology also recognises an entity that observes these phenomena, that the scientists conducting these experimenters usually call 'O' (for observer). I prefer the good old neurological term 'sensations' to the philosopher's murky term 'qualia'. 'Qualia' are defined as *'what it is like* to have a certain experience'. A sensation, in contrast, is simply *what* we experience—an introspectively observable fact of nature. Any theory of consciousness, like Dennett's, that does not start from these observational data, is simply scientifically inadequate.

The next step to note is that these phenomena have certain *intrinsic* properties that we can observe and classify. Visual sensations are contained as individual elements in a visual field. This field has a *spatial expanse* (in phenomenal space), a center, a periphery and a *boundary* (the ill-defined edge to our peripheral vision). Individual visual sensations are extended in phenomenal space, possess a boundary that usually forms of a Jordan curve that uniquely divides phenomenal space of the visual field into one **inside** and one **outside** (except in the case of such sensations as those induced by clouds, patches of fog, etc.), possess a size (i.e. the proportion of the visual field that they cover), and are colored, and may move (relative to their location in the visual field and to other contents of this field).

Auditory sensations possess location but not extension in space (except that Schilder claimed that they have a certain 'voluminousness'). They do not have the intrinsic property of color and shape, but of pitch and timbre instead. Somatic sensations possess the intrinsic properties of extension and location, as well as certain qualities such as cold, warmth, pain, vibration, ticklishness, etc. Olfactory sensations possess neither location nor extension, but mere quality.

Some philosophers of a Direct Realist inclination might object to this account. They would say that people do not actually have any sensations but we are dealing only with ways in which external things *appear* to us. The entities observed ('sensations') that I claim to be extended, colored and to move are really, they claim, physical objects that we perceive directly. This account, which seems to me a mere play on words, has never been able to deal in a convincing manner with the many sensations that we experience and can study (such as after-sensations, eidetic and hypnagogic images, and hallucinations of various kinds) that are not related to external physical objects, and yet which have all the properties I detailed above for veridical experiences that do relate to external physical objects. Nor is the Direct Realist account in any way compatible with the scientific account of perception that supports the rival Representantive Theory. This theory states that sensations are constructs of the representative mechanisms of perception.

This topic has been obscured for years by a number of muddles that we must now discuss.

The first is the widespread confusion in the lay mind, as well as in the minds of most philosophers (except John Searle and J.O. Wisdom), between the physical body and what is called in neurology—the body-image. The latter is the 'body' that we experience, that is also known as the somatic sensory field. It consists of all bodily feelings, touch, pressure, joint sense, warmth, cold, pain etc, as these are actually experienced. Most people simply think of this entity as 'my body'. This, however, is a mistake. Ever since the pioneering work of Paul Schilder, it has been clear to neurologists that we do not experience the events in our physical bodies at all. The body image is a construct of the nervous system. All somatic sensations are located in the body-image and not the physical body. If parts of the physical body are removed by amputation we still retain their representation in the body-image in the form of the 'phantom limb'. Furthermore children born without limbs still have phantom limbs. In cases of spinal anaesthesia or cord transection we experience a 'phantom body' below the site of the block. The term 'phantom' is unfortunate. There is nothing ghostly about the experience. The 'phantom' consists of somatic sensations very similar to those experienced when the physical limb was attached. The 'phantom' can usually be moved[28]. It will often show automatic reactions. If we throw a ball at the patient her 'phantom' arm will often reach out to catch it. Pains in a 'phantom' limb can be excruciating. Thus events in the physical body itself are not necessary for somatic sensations to occur. Only events in the parietal cortex are necessary, and events in the body influence what we experience only because of their effects on these mechanisms in the parietal lobe.

This has a very important relevance to the status of visual sensations. One of the most puzzling features about visual sensations is their apparent location outside the body. "Externality" Lord Brain said, "is the cardinal problem." But this problem is only a pseudo-problem for visual sensations are not external to the physical body but are only external relative to the body-image. Visual sensations constitute the **end-product** of vastly complicated neurocomputational processes that take place mainly in the occipital and parts of the parietal and temporal lobes. Somatic sensations (the 'body-image') constitute the **end-product** of other equally complicated neurocomputational processes in the anterior parietal lobe.

We could say for the moment that the 'externality' problem is reduced to the distance between these brain areas (although this will get more complicated later on).

The second muddle that gets in the way of a clear understanding of the nature of consciousness is the widespread confusion, in visual science, between the stimulus field and the visual field. This is dealt with fully in my paper (Smythies, 1996). It is the equivalent for vision of the confusion between the physical body and the body-image: or in more general terms, in any computational representative mechanism, a confusion between the **input** into the mechanism and the **output** from the mechanism. For the brain's computational mechanisms have two outputs. The first is behaviour. The second is composed of the phenomenology of consciousness—the events in our familiar sense fields.

The third muddle to be uprooted is expressed in the familiar 'homunculus' argument. This states that we cannot allow the end product of the perceptual mechanisms to be internal 'objects' called 'sensations', for that would require a little man in our heads looking at these sensations and, as Crick puts it, trying hard to make sense of them. Then, inside the head of this little green man there must be another even smaller green man looking at his inner screen, and so on *ad infinitum*. Since this way of looking at the situation leads, the argument goes, to a vicious infinite regress, this proves that we do not have sensations. This argument was first stated by Descartes, made fashionable by Gilbert Ryle, and has been repeated by nearly everyone since. However, as Fodor has pointed out, this argument is entirely fallacious. His objection was that, just because seeing external objects requires an internal sensation, it does not follow that inspecting images requires further internal images.

My objection is slightly different and is based on the confusion between epistemic (pertaining to knowledge) and non-epistemic perception at the root of the argument. The fact is that we have internal sensations ('internal' here means 'inside the organism') that we can observe by introspection. But the sensations are ontologically independent of the introspection—that is they do not depend for their existence on this introspectionist activity. Imagine you are on a high peak looking at the view before you but thinking about something else. Your visual field is still occupied by sensations but these are not very clear when you are not actively attending to them. But even when you are not actively attending to them they do not vanish entirely. Your visual field does not become a mere blank, or go black, as when you shut your eyes. Then you decide to do an experiment and introspect one of these elements in your visual field—that relating to a distant rooftop say. On focussing your attention on this particular, it comes into focus. You decide that this sensation is squareish, red and towards the centre of your visual field. Then you get tired of that experiment and start thinking about the red roof itself and start wondering whether it leaks. You might think, in doing either of these, that you are reading information off your visual sensations. If you claim this, then it will be difficult for you to avoid to the infinite regress. But you have made a mistake by confusing epistemic and non-epistemic perception. Non-epistemic perception consists in the simple construction of the visual field that was going on even when you were looking at the view and thinking about something else. Patients with associative agnosia possess this faculty. Epistemic perception starts when you gain information of any kind about what you are seeing. This may be exteroception, as when you are interested in the physical objects you are looking at—in this case the red roof itself. Or it may be introspection, as when you are interested in the sensations themselves—in this case the red patch in your visual field. Patients with associative agnosia have lost both these. They can **see** external objects but are unable to say what they are, or how to use them. This also applies to their after-sensations. They cannot say what color or shape these are either. They have lost their visual knowledge—hence **agnosia.** Thus the brain mechanisms that construct the visual sensations themselves are non-epistemic.

The brain mechanisms that give us information about objects (and about our own sensations) are different from the non-epistemic brain mechanisms that mediate perception, that is they lie in a different part of the brain. In blind-sight it is the other way round relative to agnosia. The non-epistemic mechanisms have been knocked out (and so the object cannot be seen) but the epistemic ones still function (even if limpingly) and the subject can 'guess' correct information about the object he cannot see consciously. The 'homunculus' argument only applies when the Self is held to read information off its sensations. Since, as we have seen, the Self does not read information off its sensations, the 'homunculus' argument fails to show that we do not have sensations. The phrase so commonly used "the mind's eye" does not, in my view, entail that the mind must literally have an homuncular eye. The mind's 'eye' should be spelt 'I'. The 'I' is the same as the 'O' (the observer who introspects) that appears in many of the experimental reports made by introspectionist psychologists. In the case of the contents of visual consciousness Stoerig (1996) presents an account very similar to mine. He recognizes three stages (1) phenomenal—which gives rise to images [sensations] (2) grouping—which gives rise to visual objects and (3) recognition—which gives rise to meaning. Stage 2 is lost in apperceptive agnosia and stage 3 is lost in associative agnosia. He concludes "...phenomenal vision is the prerequisite of object vision and recognition." I will have more to say on this topic later.

The fourth source of confusion that we must deal with is the theory held by most contemporary philosophers of perception called the Direct Realist theory of perception. An ordinary person believes, when she is looking at and seeing an object, that what I would call the sensations aroused in her visual field on doing this, really constitute the object itself, or at least its surface, or at least part of the time. Thus, it is claimed, we have **direct access** to physical objects. Gilbert Ryle in his book *The Concept of Mind* argues eloquently for this account of how perception works. We are supposed, somehow, to peer out of our eyes at the world and have this direct relationship with the external objects that we are looking at. Unfortunately this theory is completely at variance with a vast body of fact and theory in the field of visual science which demonstrates, to any one who has studied this evidence (which Direct Realist philosophers have in the main failed to do), that perception is mediated by our sensations which are constructs, mechanical constructs, of the visual mechanisms of perception. Vision, in the real world, works something like television. It does not work anything like a telescope (Smythies and Ramachandran, 1998).

To return to the brain-mind problem: as we saw earlier, the misplaced confidence expressed by many contemporary neuroscientists (e.g. Crick, Mountcastle, Changeux, Llinás) that we have (almost) solved this problem is based on a simple logical error that was pointed out many years ago by A.J. Ayer and that I presented earlier. Let me go over his crucial argument again. Suppose we have to try and relate two bodies of phenomena *a* and *b*. To solve this problem it would be entirely inappropriate merely to pile up vast amounts of information about *a*, or about *b* for that matter. What we have to show is exactly how *a* is related to *b*. In this case *a* is the vast body of information that cognitive neuroscience has accumulated about the brain including its role in affecting conscious experience and behaviour: *b* is the much smaller amount of information gleaned by introspectionist psychology about the intrinsic phenomenology of consciousness. In order to relate these two instances of *a* and *b* we have to construct a theory in which *a* and *b*, or at least elements of *a* and *b*, **both** take part. The Identity Theory does just that. It says that *b* is **identical** with a subset of *a*. That is, it states that the phenomena that we experience literally are parts of our own brains. However, the theory is logically independent of the data.

As we saw earlier, it is one thing to pile up a lot of fascinating facts about how the brain works in the living organism. It is something else to state that some of this brain activity is identical with the experiences of the person owning that brain. Furthermore, if *a* is identical to *b*, then *b* must be identical to *a*. So, if the theory is true, we should be able to find out facts about our own brains by examining the phenomena of our conscious experiences. The elements of conscious experience—our sensations and images—have a very vivid and robust intrinsic structure. What a convenient way to find out about our own brain structure, if it is the case that they are identical! Unfortunately this structure is totally unlike the structure of the brain, but it mirrors instead the structure of the world around us. How does the brain construct the vivid picture of the external world that is the visual field? How does it construct the body-image? The answer is by some form of a representative mechanism. The screen of a television set is a purely mechanical device that nevertheless accurately portrays events in the real world taking place somewhere else outside the set itself. Scientists looking at how the brain works in mechanical terms have thought far too much about computers—the epistemic part of the equation. They have neglected the role of the brain as a representative (non-epistemic) mechanism. This is not to say that computers, both digital and nerve-networks, are not very important and interesting models of some of the functions of the brain. But television also presents logical and mechanical features that are very relevant to how the brain and mind work—as we will see. No one denies that the brain contains representations of some kind of the events in the surrounding world. These codes may be of various kinds—topographic, vectorial codes in nerve-nets, temporal spiking codes, modulation of brain rhythms and others (see Bullock 1993): but that is not the point. The real question is whether these coded neuronal events are **identical** or **not** with the phenomena of consciousness as reported by introspectionist psychologists. No one doubts that certain brain events are **necessary** for events in consciousness as we know them to occur. The question remains open, however, whether they are both **necessary** and **sufficient**. I suggest that we may make more progress if we look for an answer to what this relationship might be, rather than to try to deal with vague and slippery concepts such as 'subjectivity' or 'intentionality' or 'qualia'. There is nothing vague and slippery about the intrinsic properties of our sensory fields. It is these properties that we must try and relate to the properties of their related brain events.

Most scientists accept the Identity Theory for what they see as the lack of any viable alternative. If you want to deny that brain events and the events in consciousness are identical, then you must hold some form of dualism, since this position entails the theory that phenomenal events are something over and above brain events. In this view the relation between them is not one of **identity** but one of **causality**. The link between events in the retina and events in the visual cortex is one, not of identity, but of causality. There is a specific representational mechanism connecting the two, made up of neurons and neuronal axons carrying spike trains. These form the material basis for this relation of causality. So what could be the equivalent material connection between brain events and events in consciousness?

The only form of dualism recognized in the West is Cartesian Dualism. This theory postulates that the difference between mental events (such as thinking and feeling) and brain events is that the former are unextended and immaterial whereas the latter are extended and material. How, then, can events in the extended and material brain cause events to occur in the unextended and immaterial mind? This is the famous problem dubbed by Gilbert Ryle as the 'ghost in the machine'. But even this simile is wrong. Ghosts are immaterial entities but they are extended ones. That is to say that the idea of ghosts arises out of the experiences of people who see what Myers (1954) called 'phantasms of the dead'—i.e. from the visual hallucinations reported in his book. Visual hallucinations are extended (in phenomenal space of course not physical space) and are not unextended. But our thoughts and feelings do not appear to have intrinsic spatial properties to an introspective analysis. A thought does not have a left side or a spatial boundary. So how can we postulate causal relations between spatially extended entities, such as brain events, and nonextended entities, such as thoughts? The answer to this is, as we discussed briefly earlier, that there is nothing in the logic of causality to prevent such a relation as H. H. Price showed many years ago. Critics complain that we cannot imagine what such a relationship would be like. This is a very feeble argument and is based on the Argument from Ignorance that the Churchlands have demolished in another context. In their case the argument from ignorance is directed to those who say that we cannot imagine what it is like for a mental event to be identical with a brain event. But the argument can be used equally well against those who say we cannot imagine how extended and unextended entities could causally interact. What we can, or cannot, imagine is hardly a good guide to discovering the truth about nature. On the other side of the coin, of course, we can ask how can unextended thoughts and feelings be identical with activity in the extended neuronal networks in the brain. All our scientific concepts of causality are based on two spatial entities interacting. These entities must themselves be material, e.g. billiard balls, or must arise in some way out of material objects, as in the case of electromagnetic and gravitational fields. Neuroscience can only deal with mechanisms and no mechanism that we are aware of has one material part and a second immaterial part.

Therefore, I repeat my suggestion that Descartes made an error in choosing *extension in space* as **the** criterion for distinguishing between the world of physics and the world of the mind. Some components of phenomenal consciousness—visual and somatic sensations and images—are extended in (phenomenal) space. Other components of phenomenal consciousness—our other sensations and thoughts—lack extension in space, as does the Self or Ego. Thus Descartes' criterion is really draws a distinction between two parts of someone's phenomenal consciousness itself. Descartes was right in recognizing that the mind has its own existence separate from the brain, but he drew the line of difference at the wrong place. So we can now raise the question 'What are the spatial and topological relations between the phenomenal space of consciousness and the space of the public physical world?'

The problem is basically one of mathematics. Nerve net theory depends heavily on the sophisticated mathematics of abstract multidimensional vector or phase spaces based in the final analysis on Cartesian co-ordinate systems. These can only deal with spatio-temporally ordered events. They cannot deal with immaterial, unextended spirits. It is of course logically possible that there might be such immaterial, unextended spirits. It is also logically possible that such spirits could have causal relations of a Humean kind with physical objects. That it to say that, whenever a certain physical state A (e.g. a certain pattern of neuronal activity in the amygdala) occurs in a brain, then a psychical state A^1 (e.g. a feeling of dread) occurs in the Cartesian mind attached to that brain. One is simply dealing with a regular temporal concomitance. Since Hume reduced all causal relations to mere temporal concomitance, then this type of causal relation (between an extended and an unextended entity) is just as valid as the more usual kind scientists are used to i.e. that holding between two extended entities. The key scientific point is whether it is correct, in an introspective analysis of the phenomena of consciousness, to hold that all contents of consciousness lack extension in space. Note that I have chosen 'extension in space' here, as it is not meaningful to ask of an introspective report as to whether what is being examined is 'material' or 'immaterial'. Phenomenal objects have certain intrinsic properties observable by introspection (such as — for vision — shape, size and location) but these do not include being 'material' or 'immaterial'. Those terms belong to a different level of explanation.

Put in this way, we can certainly claim that thoughts lack extension in space. However, there is a much more important point here, which is that, unlike thoughts, other contents of phenomenal consciousness — i.e. our visual and somatic sensations (as we have discussed earlier) **are** extended in space. A simple little visual after-image has extension. It covers a certain proportion of the spatial visual field. It has a spatial boundary. It has topological properties, as we saw earlier, in that this boundary forms a Jordan curve that separates the phenomenal space of the visual field uniquely into one **inside** and one **outside**. Moreover one visual sensation bears spatial relations to other sensations in the same visual field. Again consider the humble after-image. One after-image can lie **between** two others adjacent. It can lie **above** or **below** another, or to its **left** or to its **right**. A number of after-images can lie on a straight line or on a curved line. Or they can form a square, a circle, a spiral, etc. etc.

As I argued earlier, the visual field, and to some extent the somatic sensory field, has an internal spatio-temporal **structure**. The solution to the mind-brain problem lies, I suggest, in realizing that we can relate this structure to the structure of the brain by means of ordinary mathematics. A particular phenomenal consciousness is not a formless 'spirit'—equivalent to the mathematical concept of a point. It is a spatio-temporal system in its own right and located in its own space, a *different space* from the space of the physical world. It lies topologically and cosmologically outside the physical world (as understood by contemporary physics). Note also that people often talk about the relation of consciousness and the brain. However, this formulation is potentially misleading, since there is no such entity as "consciousness". There is only my consciousness, your consciousness, Joe's consciousness, Mary's consciousness, and so on. A consciousness is as much a part of a particular person as is an arm or leg.

The Stanford cosmologist Andrei Linde has suggested that consciousness has its own degrees of freedom and has an ontological status fully equivalent to those possessed by matter and by space-time. In geometrical terms this means that the space of consciousness is ontologically independent of the space of the public physical world. In other words, in order to describe the location of, say, an after-image in the cosmos relative to the rest of the cosmos, one needs, as Bertrand Russell (1948) suggested many years ago, a space of six dimensions—three for this phenomenal space and three for physical space. In his words—

> "An even more serious error, committed not only by common sense but also by many philosophers, consists in supposing that the space in which

perceptual experiences are located can be identified with the inferred space of physics, which is inhabited mainly by things which cannot be perceived. The coloured surface that I see when I look at a table has a spatial position in the space of my visual field... The table as a physical object consisting of electrons, positrons and neutrons, lies outside my experience, and if there is a space which contains both it and my perceptual space, then in that space the physical table must be wholly external to my perceptual space. This conclusion is inevitable if we accept the view as to the physical causation of sensations which is forced on us by physiology...All this, I say, has long been a commonplace, but it has a consequence that has not been adequately recognised, namely that the space in which the physical table is located must also be different from the space that we know by experience."

If one wants to think in terms of 'material' and 'immaterial' then Descartes' 'ghost' becomes just as material as its brain. 'Material' means only a system of causally interconnected events extended in a space-time. This theory suggests that the real Universe is much larger than contemporary cosmology recognises. It may be composed of one series of events located in public physical space e.g. in stars, brains and atoms, made of 'world stuff' if you like, as well as a second series of events located in a private phenomenal space of an individual consciousness e.g. in that particular visual field, somatic sensory field and related image fields, all made of 'mind stuff' if you like that word. These two worlds are connected by causal relations that are mathematically expressible as vectors and tensors in higher-dimensional space. Moreover the concept of 'mechanism' is equally applicable to either. If we now ask "How is the visual field formed from the information supplied by the brain?" the answer may be "by a representative mechanism constructed out of mind-stuff that functions just like a part of a television set".

Science is not used to thinking about a machine extended in a six-dimensional space. All machines that it knows about up to now are extended in a three-dimensional space. But there is absolutely no logical or scientific reason why machines should not exist that operate in six-dimensional space. Reichenbach (1958) has written on this topic. In this case we have to make the proviso that the machine appears to consist of two parts that are each extended in a different three-dimensional **cross-section** of a common six-dimensional space. However, if we were a super-being with six-dimensional vision looking at this machine we would simply see that part of the machine was in one place and the other part in another place. The use of 'material' here is simply to allow the theory to fit in with our folk concepts of what the world is like. It is a derivative of the underlying scientific concept of spatio-temporally ordered events, which is really all we have to deal with. A machine is simply an organized system of causally connected spatio-temporal events. For reasons I have fully explained in *The Walls of Plato's Cave,* if we need a space of six dimensions to describe one human consciousness and its brain, then we will need a space of $(3n + 3)$ dimensions to describe n human consciousnesses and their brains. Squires (1991) says "There is no reason why the concept of a conscious mind, which is outside physics, cannot be brought into a new sort of physics." This echoes Sir James Jeans (1930) who said

> "We have, for instance, already tentatively pictured consciousness as something outside the continuum [physical space-time]...It is conceivable that happenings entirely outside the continuum determine what we describe as the "course of events" inside the continuum, and that the apparent indeterminacy of nature may arise merely from our trying to force happenings which occur in many dimensions into a smaller number of dimensions."

The situation may be modelled perfectly in E.A. Abbott's Flatland. Flatlanders are two-dimensional beings living in a plane. They have no experience or concept of our third dimension of space, which we superior cube-landers can see lies all around their plane. Imagine one Flatland (geometrical plane) now intersected at right angles by a second plane, the two forming a three-dimensional structure. Now imagine that a Flatlander has a part of his organism that extends out of his plane into the second plane. Let us call the part of his organism in the original plane A and the part in the second plane B. He thus becomes a three-dimensional organism and no longer the two-dimensional one he was before. Now imagine that all his sense organs are located in the original plane and are thus part of his A organism, whereas his phenomenal consciousness is located in the B part of his organism. His visual field in B displays, in stunning technicolor, events in the first plane by a complex televisual system. His somatic sensory field in part B forms a body-image of his A part. He finds he can move his A part around in plane 1 and so he will get the irresistible impression that he is actually totally located and immersed in plane 1. He does not realize that his visual field is actually the screen of a television set in the B part of his organism located in pane 2, and he thinks he is looking out of his 'body' A *directly* at events in plane 1. Whereas we Cubelanders can easily see that he is entirely mistaken in this view and that his perceptual world is generated by mechanisms of virtual reality the existence of which he himself is totally unaware!

I have presented this theory in more detail elsewhere (Smythies, 1994a) but I must here make the point that I certainly did not originate it. The concept that higher-dimensional geometry might be relevant to the mind-brain problem was first raised in embryonic form by the Cambridge Platonist Henry More in the seventeenth century. He suggested that the mind might occupy a "fourth dimension" of space to which he gave the curious title "essential spissitude". The next step was taken by the great chemist Joseph Priestley who suggested that minds occupied a space of their own outside the physical world.

The theory then lay dormant for another 150 years when the Cambridge philosopher C. D. Broad (1923) suggested that sensations (or sensa as he called them) might be located in a space of their own outside physical space, the two forming two different cross-sections of a higher-dimensional "space-like" whole. His friend and colleague the Oxford philosopher H. H. Price (1965) extended this idea to images and realized that there would have to be causal relations between the two sections of the world. He suggested that there might or might not be spatial relations between the two sections, but there must be causal ones[27]. I have already given Bertrand Russell's contribution to the theory earlier. At the same time I published my own version of the theory—now called the Theory of Extension—incorporating these two ideas, namely that phenomenal space lies outside physical space, the two forming different cross-sections of a common higher-dimensional manifold, that both sections of the manifold contain spatially ordered evens, and there must be causal connections between the events in the two orders. These causal connections can be represented by vectors and tensors in higher-dimensional space. So the whole system comes within the system of a physics based on geometry. For, of course, the new theory is not only a theory on mind-brain relation: it is also a theory of cosmology. In fact it is a new addition to physics—a physics of n-dimensional space. Note, however, that there are no causal relations between individual events within one consciousness, just as there are no causal relations between one image on my television screen and another image on that screen. In both cases the causal relations connecting them lie hidden in the depths of the machine.

The concept that the independent mind is 'immaterial' and unextended originated with Descartes in response to Galileo's new physics. Before that the concept was widely held in many cultures that the human soul was something material but made of a different kind of matter than sticks and stones. The most sophisticated system was developed by the Hindu philosophers of the Upanishads who postulated that the mind was made of a matter so fine and ethereal that it escaped detection by crude physical instruments. Their spiritualist descendents developed the concept of the 'astral plane' and the 'astral body' i.e. that there exists another world parallel to our every-day one, in which we possess a second body. This idea was treated with scorn by most Western philosophers and scientists because it got hopelessly entangled with the Cartesian dogma that the mind must be an unextended immaterial entity; or because these Western thinkers had convinced themselves that independent minds of all kinds simply were products of faulty reasoning—mere figments of the imagination. However, it may turn out that these ancient Hindu philosophers and their modern descendents were right, after a fashion, after all. The 'astral plane' may simply correspond to higher-dimensional space and the 'astral body' to the body-image located in the higher-dimensional (relative to physical space) phenomenal space of consciousness. The 'mind-stuff' they postulated may be invisible, nor because it is too 'fine' to be seen, but because it may lie in a parallel universe relative to the universe inaccessible to the light rays which we normally see with. Since the Hindu philosophers were not acquainted with higher-dimensional geometry, they could hardly be expected to grasp this key point.

In order to make progress towards solving the brain-mind problem it may be necessary, as Penrose, Chomsky and Linde have suggested, to expand physics. Obviously physics should attempt to explain the whole of reality—all events in the space-time system of the Universe—and not what may turn out to be merely one cross-section of it. Of course, the use of higher-dimensional geometry in physics dates from the theory of relativity that expanded the *geometry* of the universe from three space dimensions to four space-time dimensions. The Theory of Extension is a development of Kaluza-Klein theories in physics. Kaluza (1917) united electromagnetism and gravity into one system by adding a fifth spatial dimension of real space wherein to contain electromagnetism. This was accepted and further developed by Einstein and Bergmann (1938). This idea was adapted by Klein, who added four more dimensions of real space wherein to contain the strong and weak nuclear forces. Thus the universe in these theories, and in superstring theory, does not have a four-dimensional real space-time structure but a ten dimensional one (nine space dimensions and one time dimension). Einstein and Bergmann emphasize these are real spaces not mere mathematical phase (abstract) spaces.

Some new theories in physics on space

Recently Nima Arkani-Hamed and his colleagues have presented a new theory in physics in which it is gravity itself that extends into higher dimensional space. Bernard Carr and Andrei Linde (personal communications) confirm that these ideas are the focus of intense interest just now in the physics community. I quote two letters I sent responding to their comments.

To Andrei Linde

3 June 16, 2000

Dear Andrei,

Thank you for your e-mail. It seems that the uses made of the concept of higher-dimensional space by various physicists are different. If I am correct Kaluza pictured a small extension of the gravitational field protruding into the fifth dimension of real space as the basis for electromagnetism. Then Klein added extra dimensions on the same basis to include the strong and weak nuclear force. Whereas Arkani-Hamed's group picture electromagnetism and the strong and weak nuclear forces staying within "ordinary" space and gravity itself protruding massively into higher dimensions. The account of this in the Chronicle of Higher Education says that the motivation of the new theory is the sense of unease with the asymmetry between very weak gravity and the much stronger three other forces. Gravity only seems weak, they hypothesized, because most of it spreads out into extra dimensions, diluting its strength in our universe. In that scenario, the rest of the forces and all of matter remain trapped in the familiar 3-D world, while gravity roams through higher-dimensional space. The article also quotes the proposal by Lisa Randall and Raman Sundrum that "Einstein's equations of general relativity permit an extra dimension that is infinite in extent, rather than one curled up to a millimeter in size, as Mr. Arkani-Hamed and his colleagues have proposed. If that dimension were infinite, gravity would reside mostly on another brane. Only a little of its energy would reach into our 3-D brane."

However I would like to point out that the concept of "our familiar 3-D world" is based on philosophical and neuroscientific naivety. As Bertrand Russell, C.D. Broad, H.H. Price and others have made plain there is no such simple thing as "our familiar 3-D world". What there is, is one common public world A located in physical space-time (which we do not experience) and then there are (B) a great number of individual private phenomenal space-times which we do each individually experience as the contents of each individual consciousness. A and B are not identical but are connected by a representative mechanism in which the brain plays an important role. As Bertrand Russell said the space-time system of B is wholly external to the space-time system of A. The question before the jury, then, is how do Kaluza-Klein theory, and Arkani-Hamed et al. theory, fit in with this basic fact and not how do they fit in with the erroneous idea of one "familiar 3-D world", that is supposed to include both physical space-time and phenomenal space-times.

regards
john

To BernardCarr, June 19, 2000
Dear Bernard
I have a query about this as follows. It was always my understanding that gravity in general relativity is not a 'force' weak or strong, but merely represents the fact that 'matter' induces a curvature in space-time around it. So, in A-H theory are they suggesting that 'matter' also induces a curvature in higher-dimensional space? That looks a bit odd to me.

regards
john

Recently Ronald Bryan of the Department of Physics at Texas A & M University (Bryan 2000) has also argued (in line with the proposal made by Lisa Randall and Raman Sundrum quoted above) that the extra dimensions postulated by Kaluza-Klein theory are not rolled up into tiny tubes but are fully extended infinite spaces. Thus, to include phenomenal spaces in this scheme, we simply add three more space dimensions for each phenomenal space to give, for n conscious individuals a total of $3n + 9$ space (or $3n + 10$ space-time) dimensions, rather along the lines that the mathematical physicists Andrei Linde (1990) and Saul-Paul Sirag (personal communication) have suggested. There is certainly no shortage of available dimensions. In fact there is an infinite number available. Such a phenomenal space is obviously not merely empty space but is occupied by its introspectively observed contents—that is that person's sensations, images and thoughts. Thus this theory suggests (ignoring Kaluza-Klein complications for the moment) that the total human organism is extended in a seven-dimensional space-time. One part—the material physical body—is extended in one 4D cross-section of this hyperspace and the other part—phenomenal consciousness plus the material mechanism that constructs it (made of mind-stuff)—is extended in another cross-section of the same hyperspace, in a parallel Universe if you like, as Broad first suggested in 1923. Price's variant of this theory, as we saw above, was that a phenomenal space and physical space are merely different spaces but have only *causal* but no *spatial* relations to each other. However, both Broad's theory and Price's theory are agreed that the essential relation between a phenomenal consciousness and the public physical world is the topological one of *outside*. I would suggest that which of these two theories (if either) is correct is purely an empirical matter. The essential point to grasp is that phenomenal space and its contents (i.e. phenomenal consciousness) may lie outside the brain and outside the physical world (and its contents) altogether in a type of parallel universe, or universes. Both are (or include) organized spatio-temporal systems, but are different systems, related to each other by causal interactions and perhaps higher-dimensional spatial relations as well. As I said, full details of this new theory—that I christened the Theory of Extension—are given elsewhere (Smythies 1994a) and may be consulted by the reader. It provides a much simpler account of brain-mind relations than its rivals the Identity Theory and Cartesian Dualism. The point to be made here, however, is that it allows for the possibility for the existence of the human soul, as we will see.

The Theory of Extension, of course, does not guarantee that consciousness, as it describes it, survives the wreck of its brain; but it certainly makes this possible. If sensations and images, and the Self that owns these, are located in a space of their own, as Price and Broad postulated, existentially (ontologically) independent of, but causally related to, its brain, then, on the dissolution of the latter, the whole system could vanish and leave not a wrack behind. On the other hand the Self could continue to exist and experience new events generated by mind-stuff once freed from the domination of the brain, as Price suggested in his theory. The difficulty of all previous concepts of the next world was that it was difficult to locate it anywhere. After primitive locations under the earth or beyond the stars were abandoned, the only alternative seemed to be that suggested by Descartes — only an unimaginable non-spatial 'location'. The reason that we cannot imagine such a world is, of course that our visual images, with which we do this imagining, are themselves spatial entities, a fact that should have given food for thought. The new theory suggests that we do not have to think of the soul going anywhere after the death of its body. For a person's consciousness — as a small island universe outside the Galactic universe — may be in that world already. Thus we come to understand Spinoza when, in reply to the question of where does the soul go after death, he replied that there is no need for it to go anywhere. If there are extra dimensions of space in the total Universe for the mind to inhabit, then the continued existence of the human soul after death becomes not only possible but to some extent imaginable. The matter is purely one of fact. Of course, as I said, there is no guarantee that the whole system does not vanish at death. But, if there is an n-dimensional Universe as the theory suggests, then it would seem more reasonable to believe that the whole system exists so that Selves can communicate. The whole Universe may be simply a gigantic communication device. Comfort (1989) has likened the physical universe to a giant information tape that generates phenomenal existence when played through the human 'tape recorder' of consciousness. If this is so, then is there anything to tell us what after-death experiences, if they exist, could be like?

Professor Price (1965), whose ideas on this matter are very close to my own, suggested that the next world might be a world of mental images, rather like a dream world in fact, a thought that also occurred to Hamlet. Ordinary mental images form a phenomenological continuum with our sensations in the following manner. Visual after-sensations can turn directly into mescaline hallucinations, which are a highly developed form of eidetic images, which in turn form a continuum with vivid and then ordinary visual images. Thus we should extend Price's theory to include hallucinatory sensations as well as ordinary images. From the point of view of the individual a wholly hallucinatory world could be almost as good, or even better, than a veridical one: both are existentially equally real. These ideas were expressed by Charles Williams in his remarkable novel *All Hallows Eve*, by Raymond Moody (1976) in his study of the near-death experience, and by Stanley Kubrick in the closing sequences of his film *2001. A Space Odyssey*. In *All Hallows Eve* the world that Lester Furnival enters into after her physical body is destroyed in an air raid on London, is a spatio-temporal world of sensory images, very like the account that Price gives. In that world Lester Furnival has to deal with the consequences of certain moral actions of her previous life on earth. Most people regard this as an entertaining fairy tale: but it could represent cold, hard fact.

However, against this idea is the fact that some cortically blind people lose not only all visual experiences but their visual images as well, and, moreover, they lose the very concepts of seeing and vision. In fact this goes so far that they do not realize that there is anything wrong. They do not experience the blackness that we do in the pitch dark, or that retinally blind people do. Visually they experience nothing. A similar state can be produced on a temporary basis in normal people in stabilized retinal image experiments, or in the Ganzfeld situation, in which the visual stimulus is a prolonged completely uniform white field of light. These subjects sometimes cease to be able to see at all, not even blackness, which they find terrifying. Gregory has likened this to "not-seeing" what goes on behind our heads. But occipital lobectomy does not lead to loss of the Self, which has to suffer the new and unpleasant experience. Unilateral parietal lesions can lead to loss of awareness of the very existence of the contralateral body-half and indeed of space on that side altogether. PET scanning experiments in conscious humans show that the visual parts of the brain are very active during visual imagery, and there is much evidence to show that visual imagery is processed by some of the same brain mechanisms that process vision itself. Therefore ordinary mental images do not seem to be very good candidates to survive brain-wreck. But the theory holds that all these brain events are merely causally related to the sensations and images, just as the events deep inside our TV sets are causally related to the picture we see on our TV screens. In both cases the logical type of causality involved is one of necessary, but not necessary and sufficient, conditions. So it is quite possible that, in the space in which a small consciousness module is embedded (higher-dimensional relative to physical space) other phenomena may be located, just as the Greek countryside stretched around the entrance to Plato's cave. These events are invisible to us now in 'normal' consciousness which is fully occupied by portraying the events in the public physical world around us; but they may become manifest when this flow of information is cut off at death. Even if ordinary phenomenal space is created by the brain and vanishes when the visual cortex is destroyed, the space in which this is embedded (what Brown (1991) called "what lies beyond a dream") may be unaffected. Alternatively the Self could, as it were, dissolve out of its small bubble of egocentric phenomenal space and enter into some greater reality as described by the

Hindu concept of the relation between the Atman and the Brahman. Koestler called this the "river of mind" to which the individual soul after death returns like a drop of water returning home. The question at hand is not what after-death experiences *are* like, to which we are unlikely to get any definite answer this side of the grave, but what they *could be* like given our present state of knowledge.

This question raises another one: "Are all brain influences on the mind excitatory, or could some be inhibitory?" Henri Bergson suggested that one function of the brain might be to limit our contact with reality, acting as some sort of filter keeping certain aspects of reality out of consciousness. Aldous Huxley (1962) used this hypothesis to explain the origin of the marvelously beautiful hallucinations seen under the influence of mescaline. He suggested that our inability to see these phenomena under normal conditions is because this part of the mind is under continual inhibition by certain brain mechanisms, and, when the latter in turn are inhibited by drugs such as mescaline and LSD then these "antipodes of the mind" become visible. In Jungian terms the origin of the visions would lie in the Collective Unconscious, or *mundus archetypus*, as Jung (1952) has agreed. In the Theory of Extension, the Collective Unconscious is viewed as an entity outside of and existentially independent of the brain, although normally under causal control by the brain. Thus these images could represent the spontaneous activity of mind-stuff once freed from its normal inhibition by the brain.

However, the evidence suggests that Huxley may not be right here and that these marvelous visions arise wholly within the brain. They certainly cannot be explained by any effect on the person's aesthetic judgment. The observer 'O' under mescaline retains her powers of aesthetic judgment intact, as experiments have shown, and does not judge indifferent or ugly pictures presented to her as 'beautiful'. But the visions start off in the form of geometrical patterns called by Klüver the "form constants" of hallucinations. The brain produces these—grids, filigree, mosaics, spirals, etc. in response to a variety of inputs, such as a flickering light or sensory deprivation; and no one attributes a transcendental origin to these. These patterns are thought to arise from the non-linear dynamics of brain networks (Smythies, 1959 a, b, 1960; Stwertka, 1993). Under the influence of mescaline, only after a display of these geometrical patterns, do the formed hallucinations begin. However, there is an interesting intermediary stage during which the geometrical patterns become more and more ornate and 'artistic' (very like much Mexican art), in a manner that they never do normally.

An account of the origin of these visions in terms of contemporary neuroscience would run as follows. The complex nerve nets of the brain act as parallel distributed processors of information. In these nets the computing is done either by altering the differential connections in the net in the form of its Hebbian synapses, or by developing new synapses and restructuring of the dendritic tree (Smythies, 1997; Quartz and Sejnowski, 1998; Smythies 2002). The functional efficiency of Hebbian synapses varies as a function of the temporal relation between the activation of that synapse and the firing of the post-synaptic neuron. Now one can postulate that certain nerve nets in the higher reaches of the cortex can be organized, partly by genetic pre-wiring and partly by learning (rewiring), to react to subtle details of the activity in the sensory cortex—details of shape, color, chiaroscuro, etc. in the case of vision and details of tone, harmony and rhythm in the case of sound—that constitute 'beauty'. These nets would continuously be modulated by subsequent learning. Nerve nets organized in this manner, when fired by the arrival of the patterns they were constructed to detect, would fire simultaneously and send a message to other parts of the brain "Beautiful images (or sounds) present and have been identified as such". When you look at a beautiful picture, very specific patterns are generated in your brain and appear in the visual field. But your aesthetic reaction to the picture is not simply a matter of your Ego reading off the beauty from the sensations that appear in your visual field. Rather the aesthetic feelings and cognitive reactions are computed deep in the brain and arrive in consciousness, in part, along different anatomical pathways from those carrying the raw visual information that is used to build up the representation of the object or scene in your visual field. The effect of brain lesions causing visual agnosia and blind-sight makes this plain. As I explained earlier, in the former, objects can be seen but no cognitive information, or aesthetic reaction, can be abstracted from the sensory inflow. In the latter the object cannot be seen but nevertheless cognitive information can be abstracted from the sensory inflow.

It is known that hallucinogenic drugs such as mescaline and LSD act as partial agonists at certain serotonin receptors (2A) in the brain. The serotonin-containing neurons all have their cell bodies in a brain-stem nucleus called the raphe nucleus. This sends its axons all over the brain. Layer 4 of the primary sensory cortex V I has a particularly dense network of these synapses. The action of the drug at this locus (and indeed other loci) might effect the supersaturation of colours, subtle changes of shape and the imputation of 'transcendental' meaning characteristic of the effect of these drugs on veridical perception. The drugs may also bring about the construction of distributed nerve-nets in the temporal cortex, so that complex and beautiful hallucinations are produced such as "An 18th century palace that peacefully unfolds itself, room after room, all marvelously bright and beautiful, and all colored in the same scheme—violet, cream and gold". So these images may be produced by the marvelous visual mechanisms in the brain, even if they are ultimately cast upon the screen of consciousness. So, on brain-wreck, we would not enter a world populated by these particular images. A good model for this is provided by television. Suppose that you are watching an ordinary TV program when suddenly the screen goes all misty and then you see on it a series of wonderful and beautiful pictures quite unlike anything you had seen on television before. Was this due to new and unprecedented activity in the TV studio? Or perhaps someone behind you had switched on a magic lantern focused upon the TV screen? Since you are trapped in front of the TV screen—a twentieth century version of Plato's cave—and cannot move, it might be very difficult for you to tell.

However, this theory presents some difficulties for the position that everything about the brain can be explained by Darwinian evolution. What conceivable evolutionary advantage would be provided by the construction of the very elaborate nerve nets mediating 'beauty', connecting the higher sensory cortex with the limbic system, required by this theory?

Almost all the sophisticated subjects in mescaline experiments have testified that the beauty of the visions far surpasses any natural beauty, or the work of any terrestrial artist. One of Macdonald Critchley's subjects said that she had received an overwhelming experience of unimaginable art, the greatness of which it was necessary to experience for oneself in order to understand. But is it not strange that the brains of people, who themselves have no powers of artistic creation, even if they may appreciate art keenly, can nevertheless produce masterpiece after masterpiece when they are dosed with mescaline? Humanity is surely mocked enough by the Gods without this! As Keats said "Beauty is truth and truth beauty. That is all you know on earth and all you need to know."

These considerations lead to a general theory of the cerebral basis of art and beauty (Smythies, 1994b). This states that the appreciation of beauty is a function of nerve net connectivity. When we experience and judge a Mozart piano concerto as 'Beautiful', this is because hearing it leads to the activation certain nerve nets in the auditory cortex that has the right wiring pattern to transmit signals to the emotional and positive reward centers of the limbic system of the brain (such as the septal nucleus and parts of the hypothalamus) to which they project, by virtue of the fine details of the connectivity of the nets themselves, tuned, for example, to detect certain nuances of harmony and rhythm. Of course, the music could also exist in some auditory Platonic *mundus archetypus*, but this is probably not why we like Mozart's music or even why he was able to write it. For, under this theory, the composer is only exploring the connectivity patterns in the nerve nets between his own auditory cortex and parts of the limbic system. He is not reaching out to grasp the notes from the Platonic world.

Nevertheless, in the Theory of Extension, the beauty we see and hear is finally *expressed* in mind stuff (in our sensory fields made up of mind-stuff) even though it may *originate* in brain-stuff. So it may leave some imprint on the mind-stuff outside the little module of an individual phenomenal consciousness, that may become available to us after death. Even if this neuroscientific account of the origin of psychedelic visions after death is true, we could still see other marvelous visions, as described in the Tibetan Book of the Dead, but not these particular ones.

Thus, in the after-death state almost anything could happen. What does, if anything, we will all one day discover. Until that time an attitude of interested expectation might be more fitting than animal terror, blank despair or cynical indifference. After-death experience might be similar to those we have when our consciousness is driven by its brain; or they might be quite different. The state might be permanent (in 'eternity'), or temporary, or even a pause before a Self becomes caught up again with a brain on this or some other planet in this or some other universe[28]. The post-mortem state might be one of complete annihilation like we have in dreamless sleep. We might meet the souls of people who we had known on Earth, along the lines that Price (1965) describes in his own theory; or we might not. These events might be influenced by the nature and quality of our actions here on Earth; or they might not. We might, or might not, encounter some Higher Intelligence. We might have experiences totally different from anything we have now. All we can say is that some form of experience is empirically possible and certainly cannot be ruled out on *a priori* or empirical grounds Still, even the scientific possibility that we may have to account, after death, in some way for our actions on Earth might—human nature being what it is—tend to raise the ethical standards of our time from their present low levels, as Kant himself believed, and to change our attitudes towards ourselves and other people. A torturer in the Gestapo, for example, might have stayed his hand if he had had to face the real possibility, backed by the authority of science, that he himself might have to suffer some consequences in the next word for his actions in this one.

The Theory of Extension should prove of interest to theologians and Churchmen, although it has nothing relevant to say on the bulk of Christian, or any other, religious dogma. The theory should also be of interest to parapsychologists who have claimed for years that the results of the very large number of experiments that they have carried out, even allowing for the proven cases of fraud, indicate that telepathy, clairvoyance, precognition and psychokinesis are facts of nature. But they have been less successful in providing evidence for survival in spite of numerous ingenious tests. Their claims that human beings can obtain and exchange information without the use of any of the recognized channels of sense seems preposterous to the current scientific orthodoxy. These claims have been rejected by the majority, but certainly not all, scientists who explain the proffered results away as due to experimental error and fraud. However, any one who actually examines this evidence in detail and with an open mind will find this verdict hard to accept, especially as these sceptics have usually never bothered to examine the data. They know *a priori* that they are right. The metaphysical Identity Theory they believe in with an almost theological conviction tells them so. The open-minded scientist may conclude that there may be something wrong with current scientific dogma.

The Theory of Extension has no difficulty in accounting for the alleged facts of parapsychology. Whatever may be the causal system that liases between the brain and the consciousness module (which we can call psi-gamma), all we have to suppose is that this process has a 'penumbra' surrounding its normal focus of activity on the brain. Then this penumbra could extract information from other objects, and from other people's brains, or minds. Likewise, the causal mechanisms that may operate in the reverse direction from consciousness to brain (which we can call psi-kappa) may also have a penumbra that could affect bodies other than its brain as a basis for psychokinesis.

A supporter of contemporary scientific materialism is quite entitled to make the scientific hypothesis that human beings do not have immortal souls. In the past this involved denying that human beings had immaterial spirits interacting with their brains. Now it involves denying that spatio-temporally ordered events could exist outside physical space-time in a space of their own. The answer to this is "How could you possibly know?" The new theory is purely an empirical one. Whether the postulated higher dimensions of space are occupied in the manner suggested by the theory or not is purely a matter of fact. The base of the theory is a recognized branch of simple higher-dimensional geometry. I have suggested elsewhere (Smythies, 1994a) how it can be tested by experiment. Thus, since there is now a scientific theory in the field that recognizes the possibility of the existence of the soul, the claim made by many contemporary scientists that the soul *cannot* exist is patently false. The question is still open. Some scientists, who are invariably most cautious and conservative when drawing scientific conclusions from their work, throw all caution to the winds when it comes to drawing metaphysical conclusions from their theories. It would seem that a sound training in this branch of philosophy and metaphysics should be a part of the training of any scientist who wants to extrapolate from his scientific position in this way.

Adherents of the mind-brain Identity Hypothesis should also be wary of the pitfalls surrounding the use of the concept of 'identity'. An example of this is when certain philosophers claim that "Water is identical to H_2O" is a true statement. But is this a scientific statement or a metaphysical one? The answer is the latter and it is false at that. For, as Avrum Stroll (1998) has pointed out it leads to an absurdity. For, if one says "water is identical to H_2O", then clearly one has to agree that steam is identical to H_2O, and likewise that ice is identical to H_2O. This leads to the absurd conclusion that liquid water, ice and steam are identical. Similar traps lie in wait for those who claim that mind and brain are identical, for this is also not a scientific statement but a metaphysical one.

Of course, most religions are full of ancient myths and superstitions. But common to all religions is what Aldous Huxley called "the Perennial Philosophy" that is most eloquently presented in the ancient Hindu scriptures of the Upanishads and the Bhagavad Gita. In its simplest form this states that a human finite Self or Ego, or Atman, is actually a part of the Divine ground of all Being, the Brahman. At death the Atman rejoins the Brahman, much as a drop of water rejoins some great river.

This doctrine undoubtedly arose from certain experiences described by people undergoing the unusual states of consciousness so well described by William James in his book *Varieties of Religious Experience*. One common experience is the sensation of loss of Ego boundaries and the feeling of being part of some greater psychological entity. This may be accompanied by sensory phenomena, such as seeing the clear light of eternity, and feelings of love and bliss (Nirvana), and an intellectual certainty or knowledge that the secret of the universe has been revealed. Such experiences may also be induced by certain drugs, such as mescaline and ketamine, and are found in many psychiatric conditions such as schizophrenia and temporal lobe epilepsy. These conditions are accompanied by increased 40 Hz rhythms in the amygdala, a main nucleus in the brain responsible for emotional reactions. It is very likely that the actual experiences during unusual states of consciousness have their causal roots in some turmoil in the amygdala or related brain region in the temporal lobe. Our normal everyday conscious experience only manifests a narrow spectrum out of a much wider range of possible brain-driven emotional and cognitive experiences. This wider range just illustrates what the mind is capable of producing when its affairs are entirely controlled, during life, by what is happening in its brain. But when the brain itself is destroyed, any, or all, or, of course, none of this wider range of experience could be potentially available for the postmortem Self, if the Theory of Extension is correct. The events on a TV screen are normally determined by what is going on in the studio. But when the studio is destroyed the shadows of other events in our surroundings may be thrown on the screen. Seeing in a dark glass may be replaced by direct experience. We will just have to wait and see.

So to return to the mind-brain Identity Theory: this now has a much more formidable rival that Cartesian Dualism in the guise of the Theory of Extension. Of course it is quite impossible to say at this point that this theory is correct. All that we can say is that it is certainly logically and empirically **possible**. There is no logical or empirical reason why all the events in the Universe must be located in one four-dimensional space. There is no reason either why causal relations should not link events in parallel universes. The dogma that the real universe is limited to the three dimensions of 'ordinary' space and the one dimension of time, even if we unite these into the four dimensions of space-time of relativity, is just that—a dogma derived from our 'common sense' ideas about what the world must be like (i.e. the 'folk psychology' that the Churchlands have shown to be so unreliable in so many cases in the past).

Poincaré defined 'real' space as "the space we move about in". This seems obvious and uncomplicated to common sense. It would have appealed to G. E. Moore. How could we be confused about where we move about? How more down-to-earth could we get? However, this definition is hopelessly compromised. There is certainly the space in which our physical bodies move about (i.e. physical space). But there is also the space in which our body-images move about (i.e. phenomenal space)[29]. The latter is the only movement and the only space that we ever experience. It certainly has every right to be considered as contributing towards "the space we move about in". Likewise all movements that we experience in the visual field in consciousness take place in phenomenal space not physical space.

The Theory of Extension enables us greatly to simplify our overall philosophical and scientific accounts of perception. Erstwhile intractable problems, such as the status of sensations, the externality problem, the nature of representation, the binding problem, how brain events and phenomenal events are related, what the brain actually does, the status of phenomenal space, etc. evaporate. But that is not to say the theory, as a theory in science, is true. It has to be tested. So how could it be tested experimentally? Not that that seems to bother physicists much these days. Many of the advanced theories of physics, such as super-string theory, are not remotely testable. They are merely more elegant than their rivals. However, the Theory of Extension may be testable along lines I have suggested in *The Walls of Plato's Cave*.

A Very Eminent Neuroscientist told me some time ago that the Theory of Extension was "pure fantasy". When I asked him to explain what element of the theory he considered to be fantasy, like jesting Pilate, he did not stay to answer. The concepts of higher-dimensional spaces and of parallel universes are, however, commonplace in contemporary cosmology. There is nothing in the concept of causality that forbids interactions between parallel universes, such as the theory describes. The originators of the theory—Priestley, Russell, Broad and Price— were not men given to fantasy. The theory describes mainly interactions between material, extended systems based on the simple mathematics of higher-dimensional geometry: only the nature of the Self or Ego remains a problem. But this is a problem that will not go away simply because philosophers such as Dennett have contrived the remarkable feat of persuading themselves that they not exist in the sense that I feel my Self to exist. In Haitian terms, as Searle has pointed out, Dennett claims that we are all zombies. Well, perhaps people are different. Perhaps Dennett really is a zombie. His argument is that there is no one place where the events that make up consciousness get together to form what he calls the "Cartesian Theatre" (which is really the Humean theatre). His reason for saying this is that there is no one place in the brain where it all gets together: there are just a lot of parallel processing networks that act quasi-independently to direct behaviour. Which of course is quite true. However, perhaps where it all gets together is in the mind—in the phenomenal fields of consciousness—literally outside the brain. In contrast Barrett (1958) puts it thus:—

"...my own existence is not at all a matter of speculation to me, but a reality in which I am personally and passionately involved...He encounters the Self that he is, not in the *detachment* of thought, but in the *involvement* and pathos of choice."

Lord Brain (1963) said

"...there must be a self, which is in some way independent of particular thoughts, feelings and memories, and that being conscious of these involves experiencing them in relation to this fundamental self."

How much truer that is than the impoverished and prehistoric behaviourism of Dennett and his like!

It is of course true that every new idea of any real novelty and worth is treated with suspicion by the cognoscenti when it first appears. This is particularly true, it seems, at the end of every century, when scientists tend to go through a fin-de-siècle mood that everything (or nearly everything) has been discovered and that the laws of physics are (nearly) complete, as Lord Kelvin announced in 1898. Numerous scientists have made similar pronouncements today. However, contemporary Kelvinists include neuroscientists as well as physicists. Their claim is that neuroscience has proven that the psychoneural Identity theory is true, or, as Vernon Mountcastle recently put it "Dualism is dead: thank goodness". There is no more validity in such claims, born of hubris, philosophical naïvity and a failure to grasp the real scientific issues at stake, than there was in Lord Kelvin's. One of our leading neuroscientists—Theodore Bullock (1993)—has stated in a recent book that we really know very little about how the brain works notwithstanding the "near-arrogance", as he terms it, of some recent claims that we do. How very true! Not only do we know little about how the brain works: we know even less about how consciousness is related to its brain. The Identity Theory is one, to me highly unconvincing, *theory*. We at least now know enough about brains and the contents of phenomenal consciousness to see that it stretching credulity to its limits to claim that these are *identical*. No one who supports the Identity theory can have been present at a neurosurgical operation and seen the mass of pink protoplasm riddled with blood vessels that is a living brain—and then looked around at the brilliant phenomena of his own consciousness. How could these be identical? Sherlock Holmes had a dictum that said that, when we are trying to solve a problem, we must proceed according to the rule that, once we have eliminated the impossible, what ever remains, however improbable, must be the truth. The Identity Theory is impossible because it contravenes Leibnitz's Law of the Identity of Indiscernibles. This law states that for A to be identical with B, A and B must have the same properties. Nerve nets and the contents of phenomenal consciousness do not have identical properties, and so cannot be identical. This topic is dealt with at full length in my book "The Wall's of Plato's Cave.

Cartesian Dualism is another, equally unconvincing, theory. It is equally evident that phenomenal consciousness is not only an unextended spirit. What we need is a radical new theory. That is what the Theory of Extension provides. Hopefully other contenders will enter the ring. There is nothing more stultifying to the progress of science than clinging like limpets to an outworn dogma.

I have recently been involved with my friend and colleague the philosopher Avrum Stroll in a discussion group with postgraduate students at U.C.S.D. on these broad topics. Some of them have accepted the position, ceaselessly drummed into them by long exposure to modern science, that humans are a chance product of an entirely impersonal universe honed by the cruel but efficient mechanisms of evolution. People, on this view, certainly do not have immortal souls; nor do they have any importance or role in the universe other than whatever their entirely material circumstances dictate. Religion, in short, to paraphrase Henry Ford, is bunk. This is not surprising as this is what most modern scientists, as well as many intelligent, well-informed, rational lay people, themselves believe. However, rational people should not believe things without adequate evidence. It is my purpose in this book to argue that there is not only inadequate evidence to support this belief—there is no evidence at all. This all-important question remains wide open.

What! out of senseless Nothing to provoke
A conscious Something to resent the yoke
Of unpermitted Pleasure under pain
Of Everlasting Penalties, if broke!

Omar Khayyám

Chapter 4.

The present state of religion

Christianity on the wane

In the advanced industrial nations of the West it can hardly be denied that the main religion—Christianity—is much less influential than it was a hundred years ago. Cardinal Cormac Murphy-O'Connor, the Archbishop of Westminster said on September 5th 2001 (reported by the Daily Telegraph) that Christianity in Britain is moribund and that Britain itself is a demoralized society. A year earlier Dr. George Carey, the Archbishop of Canterbury said that Britain is a country where tacit atheism prevailed and that British society concentrated on the here and now with thoughts of eternity rendered irrelevant. Churches in England are mainly empty. In America on the other hand the churches are mainly full. However, in both countries, and elsewhere, the majority of the Intelligentsia have ceased to believe in Christian Ideology and at best regard it as a series of myths, deeply moving poetic myths to be sure, but nevertheless quite untrue. In Britain today there are more practicing Moslems than there are practicing Christians. Central to this loss of faith is the widespread acceptance of the current scientific dogma that human beings do not possess immortal souls or anything like them. As I said earlier, most contemporary scientists and philosophers, with a few notable exceptions, maintain that it has now been demonstrated by science and analytical philosophy that the soul is merely a figment of the imagination, a relic of ancient and discarded magical ways of thinking. This argument fails to realize one important thing. 'Primitive' people attribute 'souls' to moving objects such as trees and the wind, because of their own experience that the Self moves its body. So the primitive idea arose that all moving things have similar selves inside them that does the moving. The mistake here was too generalize too far from the original experience. This over-extension of the theory is the basis for sympathetic magic and animism. But, to show that magic and animism are mere fantasies, does not affect the original observation that the human Self moves its body. In spite of that, and in the face of the enormous prestige of modern science, many progressive churchmen tend to agree in their hearts with this verdict and try to recast the role of the Church into a purely psychosocial mode.

However, as I have argued, the conviction held by neuroscientists and philosophers that the soul does not exist is based ultimately on a series of metaphysical assumptions (in the sense used by Burtt, 1932), not proven or demonstrated, but simply taken for granted. I suggest that some of these basic assumptions may be quite wrong, and that the soul may be no myth, no wretched ghost in the machine even, but each soul may be a dweller in a universe of its own—in its own portion of phenomenal space. This is still only a speculative hypothesis and by no means an established scientific theory. But it is certainly a *possible* scientific theory and as such invalidates the claim that science has *demonstrated* that the soul does not exist. The Identity Theory makes the quite spurious claim that it is the *only* scientific theory in the field. I wil return to this subject later.

The Decay of Marxism

Marxism claims to be a scientific theory about the motives for human behaviour, politics and economics. It also presents a programme whereby these scientific principles can be put into action for the benefit of mankind. The attempt to order human affairs according to what science has discovered about human beings is innocuous in itself providing the science is real science and not a fraudulent imitation of science. So how do we know which is the right scientific system that should form the basis for our social engineering, and how do we apply it in practice? Any science, including biology and psychology, is always in a state of dynamic flux. New facts are unearthed, new experiments are carried out, hypotheses come and go. These often conflict and the issue may take years to resolve. And even this resolution provides the groundwork for new competing hypotheses to arise to start the cycle again. At which point, then, do we decide that this or that theory in social psychology and economics is the correct basis upon which to base our attempts to restructure human affairs?

But deeper problems remain. The scientific method is only capable of finding out *how* things happen. In the behavioural sciences, no less than in biology and physics, science discovers the causes of events e.g. the detailed molecular mechanisms underlying genetics, the electrochemical events that determine how neurons work, the psychological mechanisms underlying experience and behaviour, and the social laws underlying group behaviour. But science can never tell us what we *ought* to do. It can only tell us when we do something *why* we did it; or it can make generalized predictions as to what is likely to happen in a complex psychosocial situation when certain circumstances arise. But in any human actions competitive purposes, needs, desires are involved. For example: should the rich keep their money or give it to the poor? Is democracy or an oligarchy the best form of government? In other words, should all people of sound mind, no matter how insignificant and foolish, have their equal say in how things should be run? Or should this be safely entrusted into the wise hands of the elders of the Tribe, or to those who have demonstrated their ability in other walks of life, such as accumulating money, or rising through the ranks of the bureaucracy of a totalitarian party system? Cogent arguments have been produced on both sides. But how could we settle the matter scientifically? We might say that we will select the scientific theory that is closest to the truth, such as Marxism. But how can we judge that such a theory *is* closest to the truth when we do not know what the truth is? We need a theory to tell us what the truth is in order to find out if Marxism is closer to the truth than its rivals. In which case why don't we choose that theory rather than Marxism? As this is clearly not going to get us anywhere, we might say instead that we will examine some democratic communities and some oligarchic ones in an anthropological field study to discover which functioned the better. But how do we define what is 'better'? Scientific study demands that we should measure something. So what do we measure? We might say 'The overriding criterion for the success of a human society is that the people in it should be happy. So we will devise happiness scales and the society with the highest score will be the winner'. To this various objections can be made. What is the scientific basis for the statement that the overriding goal in human affairs should be happiness? Other competing overriding goals are also possible, and indeed have been acted upon historically—for example, survival of the species or of that society, the necessity to save my soul or the souls of others, the dictates of honor and glory, and so on. If it is claimed that all these are different roads to 'happiness', the answer is that this may well be true, but the various roads are so different, with such diverse implications for the type of social engineering needed to realize them and the types of social structure needed to sustain them, that no single program could ever encompass them all, and so the concept becomes vacuous.

So we are back to the problem of assigning priorities. Should we, for example, socially engineer our culture along the Apollonian lines of the gentle and non-aggressive Hopi with their abhorrence of self-assertion, push, conflict and strife—or along the Dionysean lines of the bombastic and aggressive Kwakiutl with their glorification of self-assertion, display, arrogance and conspicuous waste (Benedict, 1946)? The historical sciences can certainly give us convincing explanations of why Sparta was able to defeat Athens, or the reasons for Alexander's astonishing conquests. But it cannot tell us whether it was a good thing that Sparta defeated Athens, or whether Alexander merited the title 'the Great'. These are matters of ethics and values that lie outside the competence of science, contrary to the claims of the contemporary scientific materialists. The question "Is it more scientific to vote Republican or Democratic?" is simply meaningless. Unfortunately people have come to believe that science is all-conquering and that every problem can be solved by scientific means.

A well-known exponent of this view is B.F. Skinner who believed that the simple Principle of Reinforcement is sufficient to explain all human behaviour. He wrote an entertaining novel *Walden II* that describes what a society run along the lines he recommends would be like. Much of human behaviour is certainly shaped by reinforcement and Skinner's ideas are valuable within their own context. But the problem is that the Principle of Reinforcement does not tell us what we should program the people of our ideal society to *do*. In *Walden II* the programming is designed to produce an Apollonian society where all is reason, gentleness and harmony. However, Adolf Hitler, another social engineer who actually had the opportunity to put his ideas into practice, had other priorities. Hitler, together with many of the German people in the 20s and 30s, felt that the Apollonian ideal represented decadent, bourgeois ideas and a thoroughly Dionysean society was to be preferred. Skinner was clearly a very civilized man, gentle, concerned and compassionate. However, it was not science that instilled these virtues into him but culture. The Principle of Reinforcement, of course, explains much of the manner of *how* Skinner the boy, was taught to think along these lines and to instill these values into him. But the Principles of Reinforcement apply equally to the process of turning a young German boy into a Hitler Youth.

Skinner's claim that society can be run wholly according to scientific principles represents the last dying gasp of the optimistic ethics of the nineteenth century. Unfortunately many scientists have little understanding of the limitations of science imposed by its own nature. Almost every program for human activity has its drawbacks as well as its benefits and it will benefit some members of the community more than others. The conflict between people worrying about energy supplies running out and people concerned with pollution is a classical example of this kind of dilemma. It is nonsensical to try and decide on scientific grounds which of the following statements is true: "Strip mining should be expanded because of the desperate energy situation" and "Strip mining should be curtailed because of the desperate pollution situation".

The term 'political science' tends to confuse people. Political science is not the science of coming to correct political solutions of human conflicts. There are no politically correct solutions to human conflicts. The solution depends solely on power—whether the power of the ballot box, the pen, oratory, the threat of reprisals and social ostracism, or the sword—and propaganda. What is 'correct' for one group will be anathema for another. Political science has three functions. One is purely descriptive and gives an account of political phenomena as they occur in nature, just as botanists study plants. The second is analytical and seeks to answer such questions as "If Party A does X in situation P, and Party B does Y, what is likely to be the result?" or "Why did Gladstone lose the election of 1886?" The third is to try and look for underlying causes for political events and to construct speculative hypotheses about these in the manner of a developing science. But political science will never take the place of decisions made by *free agents* according to *values* ordered by a system of *ethics*, none of which have anything to do with science.

Marxism came to grief in 1989 because it promised, on the authority of science, two things it failed to deliver—a universal rise in the standard of living and social justice with an end to the exploitation of the have-nots by the haves. When the defects of Marxist economic theory led to the widespread collapse of the Communist economies and when, at the same time, the defects in Marxist social theory led to the general realization by the people that the Marxists had merely changed the population of the exploiting classes, replacing the capitalists by bureaucrats and the elite i.e. themselves, the whole edifice collapsed, as soon as it became clear that the Communists had lost the nerve to use the only weapon with which they could have maintained themselves in power—limitless repression.

The tragedy of our era is that a primitive scientific theory of mid-Victorian vintage, namely Marxism, attained an immense following amongst people maddened by despair, or the lust for power or revenge, and was kept going by the apparatchiks desperate to hang on to their privileges. Marxism has for long been a failed scientific theory, not only because every one off its predictions has been falsified by events—from the increasing penury of the proletariat in Capitalist countries to the withering away of the State in Communist countries; but also because *the* criterion of science—that inadequate hypotheses should be discarded—was never applied. Thus today Marxism is no longer a viable economic theory, or a theory on which to base social engineering, or even a system of humanitarian values. It is merely a failed system for sublimating one's own negative emotions (of envy, spite and hatred) and attitudes, and for perpetuating an oligarchy based on brain-washing and repression.

Many of our present difficulties arise from misguided attempts to apply 'scientific' solutions to our socio-economic problems. Cohorts of party hacks inside Communist countries and fellow-traveling writers and Intellectuals outside them, have bent their efforts over the years to further the monumental confidence trick, for that is what it was, carried out for so many years by the Marxists. The fellow-travelers were mainly of four types: (i) good people of amazing gullibility and innocence who genuinely believed the lies and were taken in by the propaganda; (ii) cold and arrogant people of the stamp of Robespierre and the Webbs, who prefer the Platonic mode of absolutism to what they regard as the messy and corrupt democratic process (who better fitted to rule anyway than the elite, as Plato claimed); (iii) or else they were like Philby, driven, for whatever reasons of their own psychopathology, by hatred for their own culture: or (iv) professional philosophers driven by envy, malice and hatred like Marx and Marcuse. It is amazing that so many young Americans in the 1960's fell under the hypnotic spell—for such it was—of the Hegelian nonsense that Marcuse used to convey the immense reservoirs of malice that consumed him (see Vivas, 1972). There are other ways besides the demonic oratory of Hitler to betray the innocent romantic. The perversion of idealism is the deadliest of human crimes.

My close friend Nicholas Malleson, son of the actor Miles Malleson, was highly intelligent and chiarismatic. He was also a dedicated Marxist, for, as far as I could see, largely romantic and quasi-religious reasons. For him, the works of Marxist philosophers and pamphleteers, which to me seemed tedious drivel, had an effect like the Bible had upon Cromwell's soldiers. He frequently told me that one day we would have to take to the hills with our guns to further the revolution that he ached for with every bone in his body. He imagined that all this represented a selfless dedication to the downtrodden and the poor. But he never did anything practical towards helping any actual downtrodden or poor people. I repeatedly asked myself why such stuff could have such an intoxicating effect on so intelligent a person. Warping of the altruistic instinct was the best I could come up with.

Human societies have a deeply ingrained tribal tendency to divide humanity into 'us' (the good) and 'them' (the bad). Social cohesion among 'us' increases as a direct proportion to the degree to which internal hatreds and aggression can be projected toward 'them'. Hitler knew this very well and exploited anti-Semitism to this end. Marx knew this also and exploited social envy between the classes. But it can hardly be denied that human societies, as well as some animal societies, stratify inevitably into classes. Human beings are born with very different propensities and talents and in any society some people get to the top, however 'the top' is defined and others gravitate to the bottom. The definition of what makes 'the top' and 'the bottom' differs considerably between cultures (contrast a Hindu holy man (Sadhu), a Wall Street banker and a member of the Politburo), but in general the criteria center round genealogy, material possessions and power. Thus, in most cultures, clever, energetic, cunning and effective people tend to rise in the social scale and unintelligent, lazy, gullible and ineffective people tend to sink. These social strata soon become stabilized by the formation of semi-permanent social classes because each class will tend to live and intermarry with other members of the same social class. Some social mobility can occur at different rates in different countries, the successful working class people working their way into the middle class and the unsuccessful middle class people ending up on Skid Row. Even in the theoretically classless culture of the United States there is a very well defined class system based, except in the old Confederacy, almost entirely upon money. But, even there, there is all the difference in the world between the social status of 'old' money as compared to 'new' money. The imperative problem for a social democracy is to promote class harmony instead of class warfare. But this is not a subject taught in any school.

Many left-wing Intellectuals are trying to achieve a truly classless society. They feel that the hierarchical system of classes evolved by nature is 'unfair'. 'Elitism' is one of the social crimes on their calendar. History shows that any human society will develop a class system of some kind, but it also shows that the 'haves' not only have a material standard of living higher than that of the 'have nots', but also that, in many cases, they feel themselves superior to the latter and to despise, patronize and dislike them. Likewise the 'have-nots' will feel themselves individually and as a group inferior to the 'haves' which leads to the various behaviours that result from an inferiority complex and to feelings of envy and dislike. Any class system exists in a state of unstable equilibrium. The workers and peasants seek to extend their wages, powers and 'rights' and if Marxist to destroy the bourgeoisie. The bourgeoisie try to maintain their powers and privileges and, if Fascist, to enslave the proles. So how can the class struggle be so managed so that the populace is not driven by negative emotions such as contempt, envy, fear and hate and so that social justice prevails?

One way is the Swiss solution where the country prudently stays out of wars and everyone works so hard and efficiently that there is only one class, the middle class, with excellent education and health systems open to all. Other countries like Britain are less fortunate and are still crippled by fossilized remnants of old class systems dating back to feudal times with one education and health system for the elite and a second much inferior one for everyone else. Britain, alas, is still very much a country populated by 'us' and 'them' rigidly divided into three classes who still dislike and despise each other to an amazing extent, compared with much less class-ridden societies like Germany and the United States.

I was reared mainly by an aunt in an upper middle-class family in the South of England. They, and most people like them at that time, not only despised the 'common' people, who they called 'oicks' and 'bloggs', but had absurd pretensions of their own, always trying to prove that they were really upper class. My aunt discovered Nancy Mitford's ideas about 'U' (upper class) and 'non-U' (middle class) ways of speaking and did her best to follow the former. But, as she could never remember which were the 'U' and which the 'non-U' words, she found this trying.

Every member of the family believed absolutely in the following story. My grandmother's name was Mary Howard Tripp who was supposed to have a distant connection with the Howard family who hold the Dukedom of Norfolk. At the siege of Calais, the story goes, one of the Howards fighting for Henry V was the first to scale a ladder set against the walls and distinguished himself in action. So, after the battle, the King said to him 'From now forth your name will no longer be Howard but Tripp, because you tripped up the ladder so bravely'. The King also awarded him a coat of arms featuring a ladder set against a wall. All the members of my family on this, my mother's side, had copies of a document telling this tale and adorned with this crest displayed prominently in their houses and were immensely proud of this connection with the premier Dukedom of England. A few years ago I happened to be in touch with the College of Heralds in connection with something else, so I asked them if this story about the origins of the Howard Tripps was true. The reply was that the story was a complete fabrication; that no such incident had occurred; that no such coat of arms existed and that the name Tripp, common in southwest England, derived either from tripe-maker, or from itinerant dancers who 'tripped the light fantastic' as we still say. The College said that the Victorians had a habit of inventing stories like this to boost their social status. They were much amused by my tale and told me another similar one. One day an American called Ayre came to see them and asked them to confirm the account handed down by generations of his family that the name was given to their ancestor by William the Conqueror, who fell over during the battle of Hastings and got his head stuck in his helmet. At which he cried 'Give me air' and when their ancestor pulled the helmet off, William said to him "From henceforth, to show my gratitude your name will no longer be (whatever it was) but Ayre" (presumably the spelling at that time of 'air'). Of course no one in the family had noticed that William actually spoke French and not ye olde English!

The strains this system is setting up in Britain are very evident for all to see. The young have few cultural role models except for debased pop-stars. The Royal family is admired only by the older generation taught to think of 'For King and Country'. The Establishment, made up of the rich, powerful and usually well-born, still has a vice-like grip on the social and business life of the country and particularly on the politics of the Tory party. The Royal family mingle socially only with the upper crust. The educational system is geared to perpetuate the system. Some social mobility is of course possible (my cousin Captain Mark Phillips' grandfather was a coal-miner) but the ex-members of the working class who make it into the middle class, often have no more regard for their ex-comrades than do the rest of the middle class. So, before England can even hope to become a relatively classless society on a par with the United States, several things would have to go. The Royal family would be well advised to model themselves on the admirable model of the Danish Royal family, sack their upper crust hirelings, and mix with the people. No one thinks it odd to see the King of Denmark cycling round town on his own. The same should be true for the King of England[30]. The need to maintain the pomp and grandeur of the Victorian age has evaporated with the Empire. The Public (i.e. private) Schools are the main factor perpetuating the system and need to be integrated into something like the egalitarian American, German or French systems. There are of course private schools in the USA but there are also excellent public ones. My grandchildren have been to both a State school in Britain and a public school in Homewood, Alabama. By all measures the latter is by far the better. It is well known that President Clinton and the many Rhodes Scholars in his entourage have less than kindly feelings towards the English as people (as distinct from needed allies in politics) on account of the disdainful and unfriendly treatment they received at Oxford at the hands of the English students who came mainly from the Establishment. Contrast this with the warmth and friendliness any English person receives if he or she settles in the United States, as my family and I can testify from personal experience.

After that aside on the particular problems of England at the beginning of the twenty-first century, we must turn our attention to the problem of how do we increase the social cohesion between all members of the society without having recourse to the ruinous techniques of Hitler and Marx of whipping up hatred of some other members of one's own society? In the face of the natural tendency of human societies to stratify into classes, how can one reduce the tensions between them?

The Intelligentsia today, as well as politicians guided by them, focus on several topics that they consider to be essential for this task. We have already considered one—racism and cultural alienation. Others are 'family values' and 'natural human rights' in both of which areas the Intelligentsia also go hopelessly astray. There is no such thing as 'family values'. Whose family—Heathcliff, Augustus and Livia, Othello, Lear, Henry VIII, etc.?

Much of Shakespearean tragedy is based on pathological 'family values'. Many 'natural' families are seedbeds of murder, jealousy, hatred and misery in general. Real 'family values' derive from the great religious and ethical teachers of human kind and not from biology, sociology, nature or connectivist nerve net theory.

There is also no such entity as the *'natural* rights of man'. This was a political invention of the 18th century. Human rights depend on political and ethical decisions made by free human agents and have nothing to do with biology or nature in the raw. Contemporary secular Western culture has thrown out the religious and ethical teaching on which its own ethical system is based. Alas, the tree is unlikely to survive if its roots are cut away.

The Christian technique was to develop a second parallel system of values of social worth in addition to the one based on family, money and power. All men belonged to the Kingdom of God and all were equal in that Kingdom, however unequal they might be in Caesar's. John Wesley is widely credited with preventing a bloody revolution in England during the period of the abject misery of the working class in the early Victorian era, by instilling the belief in the Kingdom of God in sufficient people to prevent their collapse into despair and revolution. But he did so in a manner that would not work today. His sermons were largely composed of vivid descriptions of the fires of hell that awaited people who did not accept his message. In today's secular world most members of the Intelligentsia no longer believe in the fires of hell, nor in the other Christian myths such as the miracles, the Virgin Birth, the Redemption of Sins, the Resurrection, the casting out of devils as a cure for illness (accounts of which occupy large parts of the New Testament) and so on. All these appear to the Intelligentsia as strange myths, as poetic fiction at best, as ignorant superstitions at worst. As I mentioned earlier, Nietzsche, while retaining a high regard for Christ himself—as the 'only Christian'—launched a ferocious attack on the Christian Church. He claimed that it operated solely to protect the powers and privileges of the priests, that it (particularly Paul) had totally misunderstood the meaning of Christ's message, and that it maintained a miserable slave mentality and outlook in place of the noble Dionysean paganism of the Greeks that Nietzsche so much admired. Moreover most modern secular people regard Christian theology as actively repulsive. They do not feel themselves in tune with the message that God was so incompetent as to create a world so full of pain and misery that the only solution that occurred to him was to arrange for the murder of his only son. The Abramic concept of sacrifice to appease a jealous God is not seen as admirable, as it may have done to the ancients, but disgusting.

The power of religions such as Hinduism, Islam and Christianity lies in the fact that they meet the overwhelming human need to deal with the terror of death and to provide some deeper meaning in life which biology fails to present. In the minds of many people in most countries of the world, except Western Europe, this motive is much stronger than any desire to live according to a rational, scientific account of the world. So it would be only beneficial if the potential immortality of the soul could be demonstrated by science in which case we could dispense with a vast burden of delusional religious mythology, inter-religious conflict and abuse of priestly power.

Other religions have their own systems of myths, some more, some less believable. One strength of Islam is that is relatively free from bizarre myths. When the great myths (even Marxist ones) that bind the culture together decay, human beings tend to return, alas, to patterns of tribalism and tribal conflict, as is clear from the pattern of contemporary events all over the world today (Kosovo, Bosnia, Ruanda, Afghanistan, Georgia, Somalia, etc. etc.). Once the great myth is renounced, what else is there than one's tribe to give the psychological support that most people cannot live without? Once we have rejected religion can we re-establish social harmony by appeal to the dominant intellectual force in the world today—science? Contemporary orthodox science can only return the bleak Darwinian answer that human life has no cosmic or spiritual meaning or significance. We are merely the result of the blind forces of the physical cosmos, dominated by our selfish genes, merely biochemical information processing machines whose purpose is only to survive and transmit our genes to posterity if we can. All this may be true but can this doctrine maintain social harmony and defend Western civilization from an expanding Islam that utterly rejects this doctrine (Yahya, 2002)?

However, as we saw earlier it would be a serious mistake to assume that current physics is complete. Moreover, the results of parapsychological experiments indicate that the current scientific account of the world may have left something out. The Theory of Extension suggests just what this is. The claim made by some contemporary scientists that science has proven that the soul is a figment of the imagination represents a premature leaping to conclusions. The Theory of Extension describes a real Universe very much larger and more complex than the account given by contemporary cosmology. It also allots a much more significant role for the human mind in the scheme of things. Many modern cosmologists express feelings of crushing inferiority when they compare the insignificance of our planet and sun with the awe-inspiring grandeur of the billions of other stars and galaxies in the Cosmos. This sense of inferiority may be relieved by the realization that each individual consciousness may have a universe, an extended spatio-temporal universe, of its own to inhabit. As I argued in Chapter 3, the theory postulates that what is now known as 'the' physical universe may be but one cross-section of an n-dimensional Universe of which very many other cross-sections each form the individual phenomenal space of an individual person's consciousness, as Broad (1923) hypothesized many years ago. The contemplation of such a possible Universe engenders in me at least a sense of awe such as was expressed by E.A. Abbott (1926) in his preface to *Flatland*.

The manifold injustices, tragedies and bereavements of this world promise to be easier to bear if people came to find out on a basis of rational science that other worlds besides 'This' one exist, in which they may be destined to play some role in their personal futures. Crick (1994) has stated that contemplation of modern neuroscience fills him with a sense of awe. It does me too. But, when I read a Textbook of Pathology, I am filled with dismay, and a History of Mankind results in feelings of disgust, mixed with pity and admiration for such courage displayed by so many people facing the fearful odds provided by Nature.

The Ideology of a group can hardly be better than the Ideology of the members of the group. The first law of social reform should be that any system for human betterment based purely on social policies, on the application of a purely social Ideology, is just as likely to have bad results as good ones. Koestler's Law states that the greatest crimes against humanity are committed by people determined to do good. Social reform always needs to be accompanied by personal reform. People need a powerful system of ethics to live by. As Kant well knew, concern for the possible fate of one's immortal soul has been throughout history a potent factor in determining human ethical behaviour. Of course, in the past this effect has often been bad, delivering the people into the hands of rapacious and dogma-ridden priests always ready to burn heretics at the stake. This was because of the pernicious doctrine promulgated by the founders of most religions:

> We are the chosen few,
> All others else are damned
> There's no room in heaven for you.
> We can't have heaven crammed.

Things would be very different if the existence of a potentially immortal soul were to be demonstrated by rational, scientific means. We would not then be in thrall to any priests. Each person could make their own decisions about how this new knowledge should affect their actions. But even the *possibility* that, after the death of the physical body, the soul might have to face the consequences of its actions during its life on earth, should have a salutatory effect on that person's ethical behaviour here and now.

The rise of Militant Islam

The events of September 11th threw into startling relief the nature of the conflict between militant Islam and western Civilization. Before that date most people in the West regarded Islam as an unimportant Third World religion of no more threat to them personally than Shintoism or Buddhism. Now all that has changed. Western Governments are currently, partly for their own geopolitical reasons, stressing the difference between "benign, peaceful, mainline Islam" and its terrorist off shoots. So we need to examine why militant Islam has suddenly exploded into a very real threat to Western Civilization. This entails an examination of the true nature of militant Islam and its background.

Unlike Christianity, Islam was the personal creation of one man—the Prophet. A man of great charm and personal magnetism he lived a perfectly unremarkable life until the age of forty when he had his defining religious experience[31] and started to write the Koran at, he claimed, God's dictation. The Judeo-Christian Bible was written by men about religious matters. In telling contrast Moslems believe that Allah himself wrote the Koran. Fundamentalist Christians believe that the Bible is all true because men, recording psychological truths and real historical facts, wrote it. Thus it is easy for skeptics to claim that the Bible is composed merely of a mixture of tribal history, ethical teaching (however sound) and primitive myths and fables because the men who wrote it were, like all men, prone to error. But how could God himself have made an error in writing the Koran, unless the Prophet failed to interpret the message correctly? Hence the dice in Islam are weighted in favor of fundamentalism

However, in spite of this, it is important to stress that Islam is not a monolithic religious system. Christianity is not a monolithic system either and has historically included such disparate systems as the totally benign Quakers and the utterly evil Spanish Inquisition. Furthermore the discovery of the Dead Sea Scrolls and the Gospel of Judas, as well as the realization that there were many competing accounts of the life and message of Jesus circulating for the first three centuries after his death, has made Biblical scholars skeptical of the present orthodox account. This is now seen as the product of Church officials and the Emperor Constantine anxious to unite these many different versions into one story so as better to compete with the many other religions that thrived in the late Roman Empire. The few Gospels admitted into the New Testament (Matthew, Mark, Luke and John) became orthodox, and the rest were cast aside and became heresy, for no good reasons other than political expediency. In particular Arianism taught that Jesus was in no way divine himself, and never claimed to be, which seems a much more reasonable interpretation of his mission. Enthusiasts probably added most of the supernatural aspects of the New Testament during the three centuries after the death of Jesus.

In the case of Islam, Esposito (1998) states that, unlike the Christian Church, the main Sunni branch of Islam lacks any formal priesthood, central teaching authority or organized hierarchy. (The minor Shiite branch does have a formal priesthood). In evolutionary terms the early successes of Islam were due to the following circumstances. Before the advent of the Prophet the fierce Bedouin tribes of Arabia each had a different God and spent their time and energies in ceaseless and unproductive inter-tribal wars. The Prophet's message was very simple. It contained two basic tenets. There is only one God —Allah—and so the tribes, instead of worshiping many little competing gods, should unite under the Prophet's leadership in service of the one God, and thus cease their internecine wars. This enabled them to direct their war effort fruitfully onto external foes. The second part of the Prophet's message was to adapt the Judeo-Christian teaching that one's place in the world to come depends on the degree of one's attachment to the Faith in this world with the added information that the Judeo-Christian revelations were true enough (in part) but were incomplete. God's final message to his creations was now to be found in the Koran. Therefore the Faith to be followed was Islam that historically replaced the partly true, but now superceded, Judaic and Christian systems. The Koran accepts that Abraham, Moses, Noah and the other prophets of the Old Testament were genuine messengers from God. The Koran also accepts that Jesus was a great prophet (3:40) and was the product of a virgin birth (3:46). But the Koran denies that Jesus was the son of God (4.171) since there is only one God and so God cannot be divided into three in the form of the Trinity of Christian theology. Islam also does not accept the Christian doctrine that Jesus died to save the world from sin as a sacrifice to a jealous God. Instead the Islamic doctrine of redemption is much simpler. Each person can attain redemption by embracing Islam, faithfully following its precepts and thus ensuring that he (and even she) enters Paradise in the all important after life (29.57). It is also the duty of every Muslim to fight until idolatry is no more and God's religion reigns supreme. "The only true religion is God's sight is Islam." (3.19). Islam thus avoids much of the unconvincing complexities of Christian theology. On this easily understandable basis Islam provides a powerful centripetal mechanism to increase the adhesion of a united and enlarged tribe. It also provides an effective antidote to the mortal fear of death, which in turn provides the evolutionary advantage, particularly relevant today, of a plentiful supply of warriors prepared to sacrifice their lives for the holy cause[32].

Armed with these two ideological weapons, after the death of the Prophet, the Muslim Arab armies swept out of the Arabian desert in the eighth century and conquered much of the then civilized world including most of Spain and later the whole of the Balkans. The subjugation of the whole of Europe was prevented only by the Frankish army at the battle of Tours and, much later, by the two successful defenses of Vienna against the armies of the Ottoman Turks. The grip of Islam on its empire was aided by its policy (liberal for the times) towards the conquered people. These were given three stark choices (1) to embrace Islam (2) to retain one's own religion and culture but to pay Islamic taxes or (3) the sword. A fine and tolerant civilization flowered on this basis that for centuries was far ahead of the barbaric state of northern Europe.

However, Islam has always had its liberal and its puritanical wings. Esposito (1998) distinguishes four main competing schools in Islam.

(1) The secularist school holds that religion is a purely private affair and should not get mixed up with politics.

(2) The conservative school holds that the Koran's teachings must not be altered in any way and the whole of society must conform to God's law as revealed in the Koran. In other words one must return to the simple tribal values of the Bedouin ancestors.

(3) The neotraditionalists respect the classical formulation of Islam but claim the right to go back to Islam's fundamental sources and to reinterpret them. The Muslim Brotherhood is neotraditionalist and this school tends to be critical of the West.

(4) The reformist/neomodernist school who hold that the basic Islamic principles are sacrostanct but that Islamic law needs to be reformulated. This school is less critical of the West.

From very early days Islamic teachings have also formed the basis of terrorism. The Kharijites were the first radical dissidents in Islam. They practiced a rigorous puritanism and religious fundamentalism and interpreted the Koran literally and absolutely. In later years the original Assassins were a terrorist Shiite sect who murdered many Sunni Moslems. It should be stated that Christianity also has a bloody history with much fierce persecutions of its own heretics, the Crusades, which were mainly pirate raids directed at the Muslim world (and once at Christian Byzantium, which was sacked by the Venetians); and innumerable pogroms of the Jews. However, the main difference between Christianity and Islam is that the early Christian martyrs achieved martyrdom by dying in defense of their faith without harm to others. In contrast, Muslims achieve martyrdom by dying in order to kill infidels.

The Koran itself is somewhat ambiguous with respect to terrorism. On the one hand it says, "Fight for the sake of God those that fight against you, but do not attack them first. God does not love the aggressor " (2.189) and "...if anyone attacks you, attack him as he attacked you." (2.190). On the other hand it says "When you meet the unbelievers in the battlefield strike off their heads and, when you have laid them low, bind your captives firmly. Then grant them their freedom or take ransom from them, until war shall lay down her burdens." (47:1) and "Believers, do not make friends with any but your own people. They will spare no pains to corrupt you. They desire nothing but your ruin." (3.118). "Believers, take neither the Jews nor the Christians for your friends." (5.51) "We will put terror into the hearts of the unbelievers." (3.148). The Koran's attitude towards Christians and Jews is also somewhat ambiguous. Section 5.64 states "Believers, Jews, Sabaeans and Christians—whoever believes in God and the last day and does what is right—shall have nothing to fear or regret" and "Be courteous when you argue with the people of the Book,..." (29:46). On the other hand in numerous passages (e.g. 5.75) it states that Jews and Christians, although they had received God's instructions, failed in their duties by not keeping the covenant and are destined for hell fire. Certainly, historically the Jews were treated much better in the Muslim Empire than anywhere in Europe until the Enlightenment.

So why has the terrorist branch of Islam suddenly exploded into life? Terrorism arises from a cauldron of seething negative emotions, such as hatred and envy. The group Gestalt of being one of a Holy Band of Brothers dedicated to a Just Cause reinforces it. All personal fears and conflicts vanish in the holy glow of fanaticism. In particular, terrorism is likely to be generated in people who have been subjected to contempt and derision. I quoted Rousseau earlier "It is true that in France Socrates would not have drunk the hemlock, but he would have drunk a potion infinitely more bitter, of insult, mockery and contempt a hundred times worse than death." (Rousseau, 1973)—and I would add a hundred times worse than mere material exploitation. Upon the collapse of the last Islamic world power—the Ottoman Empire—almost all of the Muslim countries were either taken over by the colonial Empires of Britain, France and Italy or had already been taken over as in the case of what are now Pakistan (Britain) and Indonesia (Holland). Islam was reduced to the derided religion of a bunch of despised natives.

In many Muslim countries after World War II the grip of the colonial system was replaced by puppet regimes put in place by the departing colonial powers to protect their own colonists (as in Algeria and Libya), the interests of the international oil companies (as in Persia, Iraq and Saudi Arabia), or their own geopolitical interests (as in the case of Egypt and the Suez canal). Eventually, in many cases, these puppet regimes were evicted, but were replaced by quasi-secular and not fundamentalist regimes (except in the case of Iran where the new regime was in any case of the minority Shiite sect). To add insult to injury, when the fundamentalist Islamic party in Algeria was democratically elected, it was prevented from forming a government by ruthless suppression by the Francophilic army with hardly a cheep of protest in the West.

The return of the Jews in any numbers to mainly Moslem Palestine, after an absence of two thousand years, and then the establishment of a Zionist state on the land so occupied, is an episode in the 2000 year old problem of two these cultures (Jews versus Philistines, Amelekites, Canaanites, etc.) competing for the same space. Israelis are divided on how to handle this issue. The peace party recognizes the right of the Palestinians to form their own state in the West Bank and the Gaza strip. The difficulty with this policy is that it depends on the guarantee by the Arabs that Israel has the right to exist. No Israeli Government in their right minds could accept such a guarantee from existing Arab governments, which are mostly vicious and unstable tyrannies of one kind or another. The Jewish religious fundamentalist parties claim that God gave the whole of Palestine to Moses and that all the Arabs should therefore leave. The policy of planting new Jewish settlements on Palestinian land is based on this doctrine. Alas, the present policy of Israel ignores the sound advice of Machiavelli and vacillates fatally between these two incompatible polices, either one of which pursued alone would lead eventually to peace and stability. The attempt to combine them can only lead, as Machiavelli put it, to ruin.

The pressure of all this contempt and exploitation eventually resulted in feelings of outrage in many young and idealistic students in Islamic countries, in particular Algeria, Egypt, Palestine, Pakistan and Saudi Arabia. Their own governments came to be seen as servile agents of international capitalism. They felt that the wealth of their oil fields flowed to a few obscenely wealthy Sheiks and to the Power that kept these regimes in place. [33] They resented what they saw as degenerate Western films, television and culture in general flooding into their own countries. Most Moslem countries outside OPEC are still a part of what we call "the third World". It is always easier to blame others for one's poverty. Unscrupulous leaders will always lay the blame for their own mismanagement at the door of rich countries, and will spare no propaganda efforts to transmute the misery of their own people into envy for the inhabitants of more fortunate countries. Many Moslems emigrating to Britain, France and the United States have felt alienated and despised in their new country. However, this alienation is mostly their own fault. People who want to live in your country and refuse to assimilate to its culture will always be regarded as the aliens they have chosen to be. In all the recent race riots in Britain only Muslims have been involved. In contrast, the Hindus emigrating to Britain soon blended smoothly with British culture[34].

Terrorism evolved in Ireland in the form of the Irish Republican Army as a direct result of the centuries of diabolical English repression in particular the plantation of Ulster. During this time the native Catholics of Ulster were systematically evicted from their land that was doled out by James I to his lowland Scots and English soldiers. Since then the Catholics were ill treated, and more importantly despised, by the Protestant invaders. The jokes in Punch during the 19th century always depicted the Irish as despicable ne'er-do-wells.

In the South, after the English government was evicted in 1922 following a brisk little civil war, the Catholics and Protestants have lived together perfectly amicably. My English Protestant father retired to County Kerry in 1947 and lived there for 27 years without the faintest trace of any difficulty. In Ulster, however, history ensures that sectarian hatred still runs deep and is likely to remain so for an appreciable time to come. After all, it took the Welsh, who are the descendents of the Roman Britons, many centuries to forgive the injuries done to them by the invading Anglo-Saxons.

In Germany the Nazis, with their policy of state terrorism, rose to power mainly because of the anger felt by many Germans at the unfair treatment meted out to them at Versailles. What they saw as an honorable armistice, was treated by the Allies as an ignoble surrender to be exploited to the full. The collapse of the mark and the Great Depression certainly caused the Germans to lose their savings and to live in comparative poverty. But the real driving force behind the Third Reich was the bitter resentment of being treated with contempt by the victorious allies.

The eradication of terrorism in Ireland has proven enormously difficult even given the close cultural and ethical bonds between the warring factions. How much more difficult therefore is it likely to prove to put an end to the terrorism of fundamentalist Islam where there are vast cultural, ethical, political and economic divisions between "us" and "them". At least the 9/11 Commission has at last diagnosed the problem correctly. As David Brooks comments in the New York Times (July 24th, 2004) on their report "We're not in the middle of a war on terror, they note. We're not facing an axis of evil. Instead, we are in the midst of an ideological conflict....We've had an investigation into our intelligence failures; we now need a commission to analyze our intellectual failures." It is the aim of this book to do just that in as wide a context as possible.

The neurobiological basis of religious activity: is God love?

It has been well established that some people suffering from temporal lobe epilepsy (TLE) undergo a variety of experiences similar to those reported by religious prophets, saints and mystics. The principle components of these experiences consist of ecstatic emotions, a conviction that one has discovered the secret of the cosmos, and a sense that one has had a personal meeting with God. In other words, there are emotional, cognitive and interpersonal components to the experiences that have played a key role in the development of all religions. The interesting problem to be addressed is what might be the neurological foundations of this phenomenon?

Ramachandran (1998) has suggested two possibilities. Either the brain has circuits that were evolved for some other function and have been newly adapted for this purpose. Or the brain has evolved new circuits for the purpose of generating these events. The former seems the more likely. Therefore we have to ask what these circuits might be. This question can be approached in two ways. (i) How does TLE produce these psychological symptoms? And (ii) what brain events are activated during religious experiences, or more generally, in religiously inclined people?

The medial temporal lobe consists of both neocortex and allocortex, as well as two subcortical structures, the amygdala and hippocampus. Temporal lobe cortex is concerned with higher polysensory functions, memory and higher limbic emotions. The amygdala is a key part of the limbic system and modulates emotions, particularly fear, as part of a circuit that includes the orbitofrontal lobe and the hypothalamus. The hippocampus is concerned with a variety of functions including memory and some aspects of emotion. These structures do not operate by themselves, but only components of multiple distributed networks and neural circuits, that link cortex, thalamus, hippocampus, amygdala, striatum, and hypothalamus

In TLE the overactive neurons of the medial temporal lobe generate the psychological disorders described above. Persinger (1983) suggested that "Mystical and religious experiences are hypothesized to be evoked by transient electrical microseizures within deep structures of the temporal lobe." Wuerfel et al. (2004) report that their functional magnetic resonance imaging (fMRI) studies in 33 patients with refractory epilepsy this religiosity was quantitatively associated with reduction in size of the right hippocampus. The religiosity might be due to the loss of right hippocampal function and a resulting unbalanced activity of the left hippocampus. Or it might be a result of abnormal epileptic activity generated by damaged neurons in a sclerotic right hippocampus.

Ramachandran (1998) has found that cases of TLE show abnormal galvanic skin responses (GSRs). This test measures skin electrical resistance that alters in response to strong emotions, either positive or negative. Stimuli with emotional salience (significance) evoke a powerful augmentation of the GSR. This is mediated by the limbic system. He reports that cases of TLE have strong responses specifically to religious icons and words, not shown by normal controls. Somehow the excess activity of certain neurons in the temporal lobe has altered the effect of religious stimuli on the emotional mechanisms of the limbic system. The temporal cortex also contains the symbolic and language areas of the brain (Broca's and Wernicke's areas). Religious activity is much taken up with symbolism. Perhaps the overactive limbic circuits in TLE somehow induce religious symbols and words with the salience that is normally imparted only by the ordinary sensory input conveying evangelical messages. The particular religious symbols are religion specific. Obviously there is nothing salient about the geometrical figure of a cross. Such salience is only acquired when the geometrical figure becomes linked into a cognitive schema that involves powerful emotions and theological propaganda. Presumably, in TLE this process must involve the promotion of previous subliminal activation of this system above a certain threshold so that definite religious ideation and behaviour emerge.

TLE can also be associated with compulsive hypergraphia on religious subjects. Such patients commonly produce vast tomes of religious dissertations often illustrated with many religious symbols. These symptoms also fit in with a postulated disturbance near the language areas in the temporal cortex.

Previc (2006) has recently reviewed neuropsychological and fMRI data particularly in the area of deep meditation. This evidence suggests that religious activity is particularly associated with ventral temporal and frontal cortical regions and activation of dopaminergic mechanisms. Ozkara et al. (2004) report an interesting case of a 25-year old girl with intractable complex partial seizures originating from a right mesial temporal focus and hippocampal sclerosis. Her symptoms included the repetition of certain religious statements and complex kissing behaviour.

Another study has investigated temporal lobe functions in people who report 'near-death' experiences. Britton and Bootzin (2004) found that such people have a significantly increased incidence of epileptiform EEG activity (lateralized to the left hemisphere) relative to normal controls, as well as a significantly higher incidence of actual symptoms of TLE. These subjects also had abnormal sleep patterns, showing a shorter duration of sleep and delayed REM sleep onset.

So what normal brain functions could be the basis if religious activity? One obvious candidate is romantic love. Freud (1927) has shown that religious ideation develops particularly for the transference of feelings of love and dependency from parents normal to infancy to an imaginary Father in Heaven as one grows up into a dangerous and threatening world. One facet of the many faces of religion is intense love focused on one supernatural person i.e. God, plus reverence for icons of that person. Human life is driven largely (but not completely) by our selfish genes and by the processes of reinforcement. Much positive reinforcement derives from religion: warm and comforting feelings of being loved and protected in a dangerous world, loss of fear of death, help from the hills in response to prayer in difficult times, etc.. Likewise, romantic love for another real person (usually of the other sex) exhibits the same intense concentration on the other and related positive reinforcements. These feelings can be triggered by icons of the other, such as letters, photographs, and even, as in Victorian times, locks of hair. The state of being in love has many physiological accompaniments, such as sighing like a furnace. The evolutionary significance of love is clear enough with foci on reproduction at a genetic level to spread the selfish genes by facilitating mate choice and conserving the time and energy available (Fisher et al. 2005). At a social level, romantic love increases the chances that there will be someone around to look after us in our old age, and enlarges the protective tribe.

Several studies have been carried out on the brain function of people in a state of being in love. Bartels and Zeki (2000) carried out fMRI studies on 17 subjects, who were deeply in love, whilst they were looking at pictures of their loved ones, and, as controls, matched others. This resulted in activation restricted to foci in bilateral medial insula, anterior cingulate cortex, the striatum and hypothalamus. Deactivation was observed in the posterior cingulate gyrus, amygdala and various cortical areas (right prefrontal, parietal and middle temporal). (The cingulate gyrus is made up of a complex series of specialized areas each processing a different aspect of emotion and motivation). Bartels and Zeki (2004) next studied maternal love in mothers looking at pictures of their own and other babies. This activated many of the same areas as did romantic love, except for the hippocampus and hypothalamus. In addition, there was activation of the lateral orbital frontal cortex, and periaqueductal grey (that is related *inter alia* to mothering behaviour) not seen in romantic love. In both conditions there was activation in a variety of smaller areas rich in receptors for oxytocin and vasopressin that are known to mediate social bonding. The authors concluded that romantic and maternal love are associated with activation of reward 'pull' circuits in the brain, that mediate pleasurable feelings and bonding, and with inhibition of 'push' circuits, that mediate critical (negative) social assessments and negative emotions.

A similar fMRI study is reported by Aron et al. (2005) and Fisher et al. (2005) on 10 women and 7 men intensely 'in love' whilst looking at photos of loved ones versus controls. Activation was observed, specifically by photos of loved ones, in the dopamine-rich areas of the (R) ventral tegentum and medial caudate nucleus that mediate positive reinforcement. In addition activation of the (L) ventral tegmental area was associated with facial attractiveness scores. Activation of the (R) anteromedial caudate correlated with measures of the intensity of the romantic passion. The authors concluded that romantic passion is mediated by a number of different parallel processing systems in the limbic system that mediate different aspects of this complex phenomenon.

Esch and Stefano (2005) observe that love is based on a complex neurobiological process that integrates *inter alia* trust, belief, pleasure and reward activities. These processes critically involve oxytocin, vasopressin, dopamine and serotonin signaling as well as a contribution by endorphin and related mechanisms coupled to nitric oxide autoregulatory pathways,

Other neurochemical mechanisms may be involved in romantic love. The hypothalamus produces an endogenous inhibitor of $Na^+ K^+$-ATPase called digoxin. Kurup and Kurup (2003) found that people with a prediliction to fall in love had low digoxin levels and increased Na^+K^+-ATPase activity, as well as decreased levels of tryptophan metabolites and increased levels of tyrosine metabolites. Forming social bonds also reduces activity in the HPA axis presumably as a result of decreased stress (Carter 1998).

The serotonin (5HT) system may also be involved in religious activity. Drugs such as LSD, dimethyltryptamine and psilocybin, that can induce 'mystical' experiences, are partial agonists at 5HT (2A) receptors. Moreover Borg et al. (2003), using PET methods, studied brain 5HT (1A) receptor density in 15 normal males. They then administered personality tests and found that the level of serotonin binding varied inversely with the scores for 'self-transcendance', a personality trait that covers religious behaviour and attitudes. Thus high levels of activity at 5HT (2A) receptors, and low levels of activity at 5HT (1A) receptors, correlate in normal subjects with religious activity. I know of no studies of this system in romantic love.

The sense of having discovered the ultimate meaning of the universe reported in cases of TLE is akin to the feeling of absolute mental clarity and certainty induced by the massive release of dopamine triggered by cocaine. Perhaps this certainty induced by excess dopamine release in TLE, and in natural religious states, may account for the tenacity of religious belief systems in the face of all the arguments that can be brought against them.

Najib et al. (2004) studied the neural effects of the loss of romantic love by fMRI methods in nine women, whose love affairs had been broken up. Interestingly, they found in these subjects increased activity in posterior brain areas (posterior temporo-parietal and occipital cortices). Decreased activity was more prominent in anterior and left-sided areas including temporal cortex, dorsal and ventral anterior cingulate/prefrontal cortex, insula, thalamus, striatum and anterior brain stem.

Other features of religion can be explained by evolutionary psychology. For example the institution of sacrifice to the gods is usually thought of as representing a conscious strategy of trying to placate a jealous god with bribes. However, it seems more likely to derive from the much earlier propitiary strategy used by submissive males in a monkey colony towards dominant males of offering them a portion of food in the hope of avoiding further beatings. Religious ceremonies, rites and rituals can be explained by the powerful effect of theatre on our emotions, and by the calming effect of the familiar on our nerves.

To trace the neurobiological roots of these experiences is not to denigrate them. Whatever their origin, these experiences often have beneficial psychological consequences. Many subjects report a better attitude towards other people and the cosmos in general, and exhibit improved behaviour patterns in their lives, as recorded by William James (2004), Bucke (1991), Tyrrell (1946), Raynor C. Johnson (1953) and others. Their possible historical role in the architects of religions is more controversial (Brorson and Brewer 1988; Landsborough, 1987; Freemon 1976).

In conclusion, we can note that the data reviewed in this paper fails to reveal any high degree of correlation between the brain mechanisms underlying romantic love and those underlying religious activity. The former seems to involve increased activity in mainly lower level limbic structures, such as the insula, caudate, putamen ventral tegmental area and others, related to bonding and reinforcement mechanisms. In the Bartels and Zeki study higher cortical areas were mostly inhibited. Certainly there is no clear evidence linking romantic love specifically to structures in the medial temporal lobe. However, in all these studies the subjects were already deeply in love. It seems not unreasonable to suggest that higher temporal lobe structures may be required for the process of falling in love, whereas, once established, love can be maintained by lower level mechanisms. Clearly more research is needed on this fascinating problem. For example, it would be interesting to repeat Ramachandran's GSR studies on priests, rabbis and mullahs, who might be expected to react to specific religious symbols; to study by fMRI methods people actually falling in love; and to study in cases of TLE the physiological and biochemical changes found in people in love.

For in and out, above, about, below,
'Tis nothing but a Magic Shadow-show,
Play'd in a Box whose candle is the Sun,
Round which we phantom Figures come and go.

Omar Khayyám

CHAPTER 5.

The psychology of reductionist ideology: the road to Auschwitz

This chapter will explore the nature of reductionism and the Ideology it gives rise to. These factors are of course diverse and complex and the following analysis is not necessarily complete. I will discuss in turn the power of deductive logic, Gestalt factors and scientific reductionism as they relate to Ideology.

One of the greatest inventions of the human mind is deductive logic and the powerfully ingrained reasoning process on which this is based. From Euclid to *Principia Mathematica* this beautiful and elegant system has been developed, codified and its many links to mathematics explored. The system works essentially as follows. One first sets up a series of self-evidently true statements or axioms. Then one builds up another series of statements called theorems by operating on the axioms with a set of rules of the form 'if a = b, and b = c, then a = c'. The whole system depends on the truth of the axioms, which form the linchpin and bed-rock. Thus the human mind develops a marked preference for systems of thought that are based on a few certain facts, or on certainly true statements. This includes systems of Ideology as well as logic. The great hold of religious dogma and Communist theory on fanatical believers are cases in point. Likewise, when considering how one should take the

myriad ethical decisions of our daily lives, it is much easier to
have one over-riding rule that applies to all circumstances — for
example the party line is always right — than to have to struggle
with all the conflicting possibilities in a pluralist society. Hence
fanatical and totalitarian systems come to dominate society
all too easily because of the painful requirements for effort,
self-discipline and hard intellectual and emotional work that
are needed to live as a free agent in an open society. It is much
easier to base everything on a few certainties than on multiple
interacting probabilities. If the leaders like to order people about
instead of attempting persuasion, then so do the led often prefer
to live by authoritarian rules, since this removes the necessity
for making hard moral choices about one's actions. The very
large number of active members of the Nazi Party in Germany
reveled in living in such a dictatorship because one could be
certain that everything one did, so long as one obeyed orders
precisely, was always right. Likewise many Russian proletarians
appeared quite happy then with — and are nostalgic even now
for — the Stalinist system because of the emotional security it
engendered. The Russian dissidents were mainly Intellectuals.
This tendency to prefer black and white rather than multiple
shades of gray, which we can call the *Certainty Principle*, is
at the same time one of the greatest strengths of the human
intelligence (when applied to abstract reasoning) and one of its
greatest weaknesses (when applied to matters of political belief
and policy).

A second important factor that tends to promote the
development of intolerant and reductionist ideologies is
the matter of Gestalt boundaries of these systems. Sensory
psychologists developed the concept of Gestalt in the early
years of the last century. The human sensory system has a
built-in tendency to gather groups of items in perception into
wholes or 'Gestalts'. These then take on a fairly rigid structure
and resist being broken up or being added to. Gestalt principles
can be applied to social matters. The simple rural villager of not
too long ago, for whom all strangers from outside his village are
foreigners to be feared and distrusted no matter how benign

the appearances might be, exemplifies the action of a social Gestalt. Totalitarian systems, both secular and religious, have hard Gestalt boundaries dividing areas in which the faithful live in a spirit of fanatical dedication, from areas from which one is totally excluded. This contrasts with one's more flexible relationship to social structures, such as political parties or Churches, in a democracy, where they do not try to be all things to all people.

These Gestalts also apply to science where time and time again brilliant new innovations have been fiercely resisted by the Gestalt-ridden old guard. As Comfort (1985) put it:

"There are plenty of historical examples of our tendency to draw the wagons around a Worldview that appears self-evident to all right-thinking men...Rash speculation does not bother the physicists—it has got them where they are today. And it is high time that life sciences looked critically at the solidarity of their tribal idols, including stochastic-genetic evolution, morphogenesis, and the 'mind-body' problem."

My third topic is reductionism itself. This is a very important concept over which there is a great deal of contemporary confusion. Thirty years ago Arthur Koestler and I edited the proceedings of the Alpbach Symposium as a book called *Beyond Reductionism*. There are, however, two distinct senses of 'reductionism' that tend to get entangled. One of these is innocuous—the other is distinctly malignant. The first, harmless variant arises out of the structure of the scientific process itself. This is arranged on a series of levels. The first level is natural history, which dominated eighteenth century science. In this, we examine the world around us and simply describe and classify what we find—rocks, plants, animals, stars, etc. The second, in biology, is the physiological level in which we try to find out how things work. For example, the naturalist discovers the heart and notices that its rate of beating varies. The physiologist then starts a series of experiments to find out what controls the heart beat in this fashion, He discovers that he can slow the heart by stimulating the vagus nerve. So he asks "Why does stimulating the vagus nerve cause the heart to slow down?" The answer, discovered by Otto Loewi, is that it does so by releasing a chemical called acetylcholine from its nerve endings. This involves a jump to the next, or biochemical level, of the positivist hierarchy. The fourth jump to the biophysical level occurs when we inquire into how acetylcholine affects heart cells by altering ion fluxes into the cells. This process is called 'reduction'. The questions raised at one level are answered at the next level. Thus one reduces natural history to physiology to biochemistry to biophysics. However, it is important to notice that this main reductionist sequence is not the only one in science. There are two other independent reductionist systems. The first deals with the behaviour of groups and include topics like systems theory and chaos theory. These do not reduce to physiology for they describe activity in many groups besides organisms, such as the weather, for example. Instead they reduce to other systems of mathematics such as statistics and non-linear dynamics. The second deals with the data obtained by psychologists using the technique of introspection. The data for the rest of science is obtained by exteroception (perception) of the external world. By contrast the data of introspectionist psychology is obtained by examining the contents of our own consciousness—e.g. our sensory fields, our images and thoughts—that is of our internal worlds. An analogy for this is provided by television. We normally use television to see what is going on in the TV studio (= exteroception). But we can also examine the TV screen as it actually is in itself—a series of parallel colored lines drawn on a cathode ray oscilloscope screen by an electron beam (the raster). This is equivalent to introspection. This system does not ordinarily reduce to physiology either but to the mathematics of geometry and topology. I have covered certain attempts, that have been made to reduce these data to physiology, elsewhere (Smythies, 1994a).

Some scientists and philosophers have been worried by this kind of reduction because it seems to them to reduce human beings to mechanical puppets. They have sought to avoid this depressing conclusion by invoking the doctrine of 'emergent properties'. In general, this states that one can never describe the properties of a whole by an exhaustive description of the properties of its constituent parts. For example the atoms of a red pigment are not themselves red. 'Redness' is held to be an emergent property belonging to the whole not the parts. Thus, it has been claimed that human beings could also have such emergent properties, such as free will, not determined by the causal nexus of the detailed molecular and neuronal events in the brain. I do not think myself that this argument is valid. Human free will depends on allowing, in our theory of humanity, a role for the subjective Self permitting it independent existence and the power to act on the brain as the originator of acts of free will. This is provided in the Theory of Extension. In this theory the (subjective) Self and its phenomenal (objective) consciousness (Honderich, 1988) exist in their own right and do not depend for this *existence* on anything else, although of course they are dominated by causal influences from the brain. In this theory, phenomenal consciousness, as a spatio-temporal complex, cannot be reduced to brain chemistry and physics, since it is not anatomically part of the brain. The brain contains the *causal ancestors* (i.e. neuronal activity) of the events in consciousness— our various sensations, images and thoughts—but it does not contain these events themselves. This is like the fact that events on the TV screen are determined by what is going on inside the TV set (and by events in the TV studio further down the line) but they are not *identical* with them. Biochemistry and biophysics apply only to events in the brain itself, not to events in phenomenal consciousness. Whether events in this consciousness are *identical* with their correlated brain events or not, is a question quite independent of the question of what is the nature of these particular brain events themselves. In the Theory of Extension the reductionist chain operates fully but it reduces to an n-dimensional physics, not a four-dimensional physics. This new physics is no longer any threat to human freedom and dignity.

The second and harmful sense of reductionism is involved when we give causal or scientific explanations and recommendations for certain complex human social and motivational systems and behaviours. These are determined by the complex interplay of diverse forces, biological instincts, emotions, economics, creativity, aesthetics, social hierarchies, etc.. Reductionism in this sense is the claim that one of these is much more important than the others and should be allowed to dominate our value system. For example, Marx claimed to have discovered that human motivation—the real causes for human action—is a matter of economics and class psychology. People manufacture the things that they need and develop the social structures necessary to do so. These are subject to the 'scientific laws' that Marx claimed to have discovered. This statement of the theory is not reductionistic, even if the laws turn out to be all wrong. Pernicious (psychosocial) reductionism is brought into play when the Marxists went on to claim that other human activities must be subsumed under the dominant one. Religion is abolished on the ostensive ground that it is untrue—and on the covert grounds that the Communists did not want any rivals as the target for the fanatical loyalty of their followers; art must portray only socialist realism; sport must be used to demonstrate the superiority of Marxism-Leninism, and so on. The origin of the Communist attempt to take over society and control human behaviour is really determined, not by the economic 'laws' of Marxism-Leninism, but by the laws of social reductionism, social Gestalts and the Certainty Principle we discussed earlier, together with the Machiavellian laws that govern all totalitarian and tyrannical systems. We must discover how a self-appointed elite can continue to fool and bamboozle the people, if not for ever, nevertheless for more than the average lifetime. Any such reductionist system will eventually have disastrous results because the course of affairs will be determined, not by the overt 'laws' of the theoretical system on which all attention is focused, but by the unnoticed operation of laws which these pioneer social scientists and engineers simply failed to take into account. These include the laws governing the development of the secret police, the influence of the actions which, as Machiavelli described so graphically, the winner in a totalitarian power struggle has to take in order to achieve and maintain absolute power (Saddam Hussein and Slobodan Milosevic offer excellent case studies here). Thus we observe the descent of the early Bolsheviks, some of whom may have been well-meaning people, into the maw of the Stalinist Terror. They were like men watching a brightly lit screen portraying a film, being gradually being picked off one by one by dark figures stealing unseen out of the darkness around them.

An important element in all this at a deeper level is provided by the emotional reinforcement of fanaticism. All personal doubts, fears and neuroses vanish in the glittering light of dedicated service, shoulder to shoulder with the Faithful, in so noble a Cause. It is we, alas, we have to pay the price for this delusional euphoria. Now that Communism, German Tribalism and Christianity, as religions have collapsed, or all but collapsed, the one force in the world today capable of inspiring such fanaticism is militant Islam. Since the traditional Western Ideology is today so feeble a force, having been undermined for the last century by its enemies, it is not difficult to see how that those countries, like Egypt and Algeria, that still adhere to a secular form of Islam, could so easily eventually be swept up, like Iran and the Afghanistan of the Taliban, into the maelstrom of fanatical militant Islam, particularly under the pressure of a relentless population explosion. I am not saying here that Islam itself presents a potent danger to Western secular civilization. As I have dealt with elsewhere in this book, there are aspects of Islam, and its non-militant branches that have many admirable characteristics. It is the interpretation that counts. What we need to do in the West is to examine the causes of the weakening of our own Ideology at the hands of the Intelligentsia, to determine if the intellectual causes for this are valid, and if we decide not, to do something about it.

Further Trends in Reductionism

Psychoanalysis

The currents of scientific reductionism that have been most prominent in the United States have derived from psychoanalysis and behaviourism. Fortunately the epidemic of reductionism never reached the extent attained in the Soviet Union, and the United States, even with the disgusting violence promoted by Hollywood and the gun myths, remains in the main a healthy society. Freud's psychology, unlike Marxism, was never designed as an ideology and never really developed into one. But the (social) reductionist tendencies in some of Freud's disciples have had undesirable effects on particular areas of American life, and to a lesser extent in the West generally, particularly in child rearing practices and education. Freud's psychology was developed to explain certain clinical features he found in his largely hysterical patients in Franz Joseph's Vienna. He made most important discoveries about certain functions in a limited area of human psychology, in particular psychosexual development and the vagaries of memory in dissociative states. Unfortunately, the forces of social reductionism operating in some of Freud's over-enthusiastic followers ensured that these explanatory concepts were carried too far outside their proper frame of reference. This extended to psychohistory, art, religion, etc. and served to obscure other important determinants active in these subjects. It is also true to say that the basic concepts of his theory in terms of psychological *entities* such as the Ego, Superego and Id, can now be translated into nerve net theory as I have done elsewhere (Smythies, 1994c).

Misapplications and misunderstandings of Freudian theories played their part in the development of the highly damaging 'permissive' child-rearing practices of the 50s and 60s which led in turn to the student revolt of the late 60s and the hedonistic, amoral, drug-oriented culture that still afflicts us. The Freudian concept of 'repression' has a highly technical meaning relevant to how one deals with memories too painful to bear. These were said to be 'repressed' into the unconscious, where they continued to fester away, leading to the symptoms of neurosis. Thus the idea was born that 'repression' is a bad thing. The meaning of 'repression' was then quite illegitimately transposed to 'repressing' one's instincts and certain patterns of behaviour. Thus the curious idea grew in the minds of progressive educators and child psychologists that children should not have to repress anything they wanted to do, no matter how anti-social. It also led to the theory that it is harmful to repress sexual desire and practice chastity since a neurosis might result.

It is certainly true that psychiatric neuroses result in part from the harmful conditioning of guilt and shame onto various substrata—instances of psychic trauma. But giving free rein to one's instincts is not the answer. The answer is to contain the guilt and shame. The doctrine of giving free rein to one's primitive instincts, plus the doctrine of the Noble Savage, obscure the fact that civilized attitudes and modes of behaviour have to be taught. In the final analysis, human beings are the product of millions of years of evolution that cared nothing for civilized behaviour. What evolution produced were tribes in which the members were ruthless, cunning and aggressive, but with a strong internal cohesion, so that these attributes were directed outwards towards other competing tribes rather than inwardly to disrupt one's own tribe. What Highland clans were like before 1745 are good examples of this. The men had to be effective warriors, and the tribe had to have the strong cohesion provided by myth, custom, discipline, good leadership, etc. Thus a child allowed to develop his 'instincts' is likely to become a savage rather than manifest the innocence depicted by Rousseau, or the saintliness depicted by sentimental Victorian authors. The Apollonian virtues of kindliness, tolerance, humor, altruism, good 'manners', concern for others, etc. are likely to whither and die in any culture which does not make it a *primary* aim of education to instill these virtues at all times in all members of the culture, instead of hoping that Nature, left to itself, will do this for us.

Psychoanalysis, as a clinical science, properly covers certain psychiatric disorders, such as hysteria, phobias and the sexual neuroses that constituted the bulk of Freud's practice in nineteenth century Vienna in which sexuality was associated with a good deal of fear, shame and guilt. But when we consider other psychiatric disorders such as manic-depressive illness or schizophrenia, psychoanalytic theory and therapy becomes less relevant, as there is today every indication that these are organic disorders of the brain. There are many aspects of human life to which the damaging experience of fear, shame and guilt can be conditioned—for example the hurt of being unloved, unappreciated, a social outcast for breaking some taboo, failure, loss of honour, being branded a heretic in some branch of belief or learning, sexual abuse as a child, etc.. If fear, shame and guilt are sufficiently conditioned a painful neurosis may result in a predisposed person. The content of the neurosis may depend in part on the particular cause of the shame and guilt. Freud was quite right to point out the important fact that toilet training is often the first occasion an infant encounters guilt and shame. Human feelings and behaviour depend on many complex factors, such as the struggle for power and prestige, the play of powerful emotions such as hatred, envy, jealousy as well as the most damaging ones of fear, shame and guilt that we have already considered. Fear out of control leads to anxiety (a polite word for naked terror) neuroses; in depressive illnesses, even if organically caused, delusions based on guilt and shame are common. Neurosis will be likely to result from faulty conditioning of fear, guilt and shame in response to whatever situations that culture determines are vehicles for these damaging emotions. Adler explored the role of the power motive, which entails the fear of failure and the guilt and shame induced by actual failure. Jung studied something else—the power of myth and the collective unconscious. For he was a doctor in an asylum and saw mainly schizophrenics in which these factors are important.

The main benefits of psychoanalysis are to be found in the cultural attitudes towards sex, which in some respects are healthier than they were a hundred years ago when Freud was beginning his work. At that time sex was as taboo as death is today. The human body was regarded as an object of shame to the extent that even female ankles were regarded as indecorous. What were the reasons for this remarkable attitude and what are the factors that have been responsible for the changes seen in our times? Major factors responsible for the fear of sex in Victorian times must have been the very real threat of dying in childbirth, the fear of unwanted pregnancies when this spelt social ruin in days when a good marriage settlement was a woman's only hope, the Christian concept of original sin, and the ravages of venereal disease. The Renaissance Church had an easy-going attitude to sexual matters. No one thought it odd that the Pope should have several mistresses and a bevy of children. All this changed when Columbus's sailors, returning from the West Indies, introduced syphilis into Europe. This proved a blow to the mental health of Europe on the same scale that the Black Death had proved two centuries before to its physical health. In a population with no natural immunity syphilis caused an epidemic. Sufferers died during the secondary stage in such horrible circumstances that the disease attracted the name the 'Great Pox', in contrast to mere smallpox.

The gradual return towards a more rational attitude towards sex may be traced to a number of factors. The slow development of relative immunity to syphilis (that still killed unfortunate sufferers such as Lord Randolph Churchill, and Schubert); the Elizabethan renaissance of the arts, especially the love poetry of Shakespeare, Marlowe and Donne; the return of pagan Greek attitudes via the great admiration of the Age of Reason for classical Greece; the whole attitude of the eighteenth century which was conducive to the rational solution of problems instead of the blind acceptance of old terrors; the rise of technology and capitalism with the resultant growth of a leisure class able to nurture infant science and scientific medicine. All this served to change the focus of the culture from the preoccupation with theology, guilt and sin, induced by helpless misery, to attention to science, secular philosophy and secular art, and to the Apollonian virtues of an advanced civilization.

These changes occurred at that time mostly amongst the aristocracy and the Intelligentsia. The developing middle classes, from whose ranks most of Freud's patients came, remained strongly puritanical, at least in theory. The Victorian *ideal* stressed the Christian virtues embedded in the traditional concept of marriage. In the Victorian *reality*, all too often, we find abundant evidence of nauseating hypocrisy, widespread prostitution, and the subjugation of women so forcibly expressed by Anne Brontë in *The Tenant of Wildfell Hall*.

The last few years have seen a reaction by many young people against the excesses of the sexual revolution, from its mindless promiscuity to its preoccupation with the most painful and unrewarding of human endeavors — the pursuit of pleasure. The ancient virtues show signs of returning, to some degree at least and in some places.

My main criticism of Freud, together with reductionist biology that sees humans as *only* naked apes, is that their description of humans, as containing within their makeup a horrific component — is only too true. The history of Nazi Germany illustrates only too graphically what can happen when the Id gets out of control. And the Id can get out of control all too easily in societies that believe that man is *only* an ape honed by the ruthless forces of evolution in which *only* the ability to survive counts; as well as societies riven with religious fanaticisms or degenerating into tribal warfare. As the history of our times, indeed of almost any other times, shows in cold, revolting detail, humans can, and often do, behave towards other humans in a manner that no other species known to science behaves towards other members of its own species. Einstein once expressed his disgust at belonging to so vicious a species. In history what Freud called the Id, what Christians called evil, what Koestler called the paranoid streak in man, can only be kept under control by a super-Ego that has the power to do so. Historically the forces of the super-Ego have come from our Judeo-Christian (and Hindu, Buddhist and nonfundamentalist Moslem) cultures. Anything that weakens the super-Ego strengthens the Id. Anything that weakens Dr. Jekyll strengthens Mr. Hyde. Thus members of the Intelligentsia, who put forward claims—such as that we know that God is dead, or that science has *proved* that the soul is a myth, or that all religion is a by-product of the psychopathology of our infancy, or that people are mindless automata—are playing with fire.

Viktor Frankl, Professor of Neurology and Psychiatry in the University of Vienna was one of the leading psychotherapists of his day. I first met him at the Alpbach Symposium in 1968. He founded a system of psychotherapy called logotherapy based on the search for meaning in life. His survival of Auschwitz gives him particular authority to speak on these matters. In his book *The Doctor and the Soul* (Frankl, 1973b) he says that the social reductionism of modern psychology—that man is nothing more than a mind-machine, a pawn of drives and reactions, the mere product of instinct, heredity and environment—leads to nihilism and corruption. He says that the gas chambers of Auschwitz were

"...the ultimate consequence of the theory that man is nothing but the product of heredity and environment—or, as the Nazis liked to say 'of Blood and Soil'... I am absolutely convinced that the gas chambers of Auschwitz...were ultimately prepared not in some ministry or other in Berlin, but rather at the desks and in the lecture halls of nihilistic scientists and philosophers".

As Frankl (1973a) says, the conversion of the scientific reductionism of science (harmless in itself) into social reductionism (lethal) leads to the perversion of truth and prepares the ground for manifold social disasters, and for the waves of personal despair, so graphically described by Frankl, that affect our civilization today. Take, for example, the epidemic of drug addiction. After decades of being taught by hordes of psychologists and philosophers that humans are only physicochemical machines, whose only objective, besides being slaves to their tyrannical genes, is to maximize positive reinforcement (pleasure) and minimize negative reinforcement (pain), no wonder the allure of instant ecstasy in the form of heroin and cocaine becomes so hard to resist. For a brief moment the person, who is no longer human, crushed by the emptiness and meaninglessness of existence, is transformed by the drug into a god.

The Government of the United States has declared war on drug abuse, which it is conspicuously losing. The weapons in this war seem to consist of trying to persuade other countries from growing the plants from which the drugs are obtained, trying to keep drugs out of the country, trying to persuade people not to take them, locking up a few of the dealers and all too many minor offenders. Little effort has been directed towards dealing with the main cause — the moral decay at the heart of civilization brought about by the relentless spread of the nihilism that Viktor Frankl declaimed against so forcefully a quarter of a century ago.

The products of the desks of nihilistic scientists and philosophers exemplify themselves in ways other than concentration camps and drug addiction. People who believe themselves to be merely chemical machines, or glorified computers, seem to be able to paint, or compose music, or write literature only in a manner that a computer might. To call much of modern art (painting, sculpture, literature, music) 'art' is to stretch the language in a manner its founders did not intend. The correct word is 'garbage'. In fact one can go further. Much modern art, such as Picasso's later work, may be technically brilliant, but it reflects only the evil and ugliness, and the bitter sense of betrayal, at the heart of the Ideology based on the ideas of contemporary scientists and philosophers about the nature of the human mind. Pop music, it has been claimed, is possibly the most degenerate music that has ever been written (O'Brien, 1989). Two cases have recently been reported in the medical press of fronto-temporal dementia that support this claim. Both patients before their illness were much attached to classical music. After the dementia developed they lost all interest in classical music, but spent hours listening to pop music instead.

In each field, of course, there are individuals courageous enough to stand out and protest against this fatal drift. These people claim, in my opinion correctly, that the current orthodox view of the nature of mind is wrong and is based on very obvious errors of reasoning based on spectacularly incorrect folk psychology, as I have detailed elsewhere (1992a). Some names that come to mind are not bungling amateurs but stellar leaders in their fields: in neurology Sir Francis Walshe (see especially his marvellous papers in *Brain* (1951, 1953)), Lord Brain and Wilder Penfield; in the neurosciences Hartwig Kuhlenbeck, Sir Charles Sherrington and Sir John Eccles; in psychology John Beloff, Robert Morris and Alan Gauld; in psychiatry Ian Stevenson and Carl Gustav Jung; Steven Harrison in the computer sciences; Roger Penrose, Andrei Linde, Undo Uus, Erwin Schrödinger, Werner Heisenberg[35] and Bernard Carr in physics; Arthur Koestler and Rosalind Heywood in literature; C.D. Broad, H.H. Price, Howard Robinson, John Foster, Geoffrey Madell, Jonathan Harrison, Robert Almeder and Roland Puccetti in philosophy. Also one must admire that rarest of individuals—a saintly politician like Mahatma Gandhi and Nelson Mandela.

Conclusion

The truth of the matter is that great and important questions, such as the nature of consciousness and its relation to the brain, the existence of the soul and the 'next world' are still entirely open and have in no way been solved, or negated, by modern science and philosophy. All claims to the contrary are based on premature jumping to conclusions, the inability to question one's own erroneous presuppositions and prejudices—which are mistaken for 'self-evident facts'—and plain failures of reason and logic (Puccetti, 1989).

As any practicing psychiatrist can testify, many people, unsustained by any form of religious faith or feeling (even an atheistic one), at times come to feel that their lives are empty and devoid of meaning. This leaves them prey to surrogate religions such as Marxism; or the worship of demagogues like Adolf Hitler; or to attempts to dull their misery with alcohol and drugs; or to catastrophic feelings of despair at what they perceive as permanent loss when people they love die.

Many people are tormented by fear for much of their lives. Technically this passes in psychiatry under the more reassuring title of anxiety—anxiety states, free floating anxiety, phobias, etc. But what it is is fear. Much of this is due to some real life situation, or previous harmful conditioning, or specific psychopathologies. But lying behind these, in many people, lies an overall fear of living and dying in a cold impersonal universe—a fear of existence itself and the pain and misery that this existence so frequently brings. Such existential fears can best be kept at bay by adopting an ideology that gives a deeper meaning to one's life and that enables one to take—to use Schweitzer's phrase—an optimistic ethical *Weltanschauung* on the Cosmos. Many sensitive, imaginative and artistic people wish passionately to believe from their inner selves that they are more than the machines that modern science tells them they are, that they embody some immortal principle of truth and beauty, that their loved ones possess something that can be called a soul, and that death does not us part. The conflict between this inner belief and the official dogma of our culture, shared by most psychotherapists, and in secret by many 'liberal' clergymen, that all this is untrue, causes much pain and anguish in such people.

What people need from science and philosophy is the truth, not speculations based on prejudice and ignorance, and dogma masquerading as rational argument. Francis Crick (1994) has recently written a book in which he expresses the belief beyond any reasonable doubt that modern science has shown that the immortal human soul is a mere myth and that all our mental existence is nothing more than the activity of complex nerve nets in our brains. I wrote two critical reviews of this book, one for a neurological audience in *Brain* and one for a philosophical audience in *Inquiry*. However, he hedges this position elsewhere. Crick and Koch (1992) say that in order to explain consciousness "radically new concepts may indeed be needed—recall the modifications of scientific thinking forced on us by quantum mechanics." My present book presents candidates for these radically new concepts. The truth is that it is certainly possible, but of course it has by no means been established, that people do, after all, possess immortal souls, that they may enter into other forms of existence after the death of the physical body, and that Wordsworth presents a truer picture of reality than does Hobbes.

BIBLIOGRAPHY

Abbott, EA. *Flatland. A Romance of Many Dimensions.* Oxford University Press, 1926.

Almeder, R. *Death and Personal Survival: the Evidence for Life after Death.* Lanham, Maryland, Rowman & Littleport, 1992.

Aron, A, Fisher H, Mashek DJ, Strong G, Li H, Brown LL. (2005) *J.Neurophysiol.* 94, 327-337.

Ayer, AJ. in *The Physical Basis of Mind* (P. Laslett ed.) Oxford, Blackwell, 1952.

Barrett, W. *Irrational Man.* London, Doubleday, 1958.

Barrett, W. *The Death of the Soul. From Descartes to the Computer.* Garden City, N.Y., Anchor Press, 1986.

Bartels A, Zeki S. (2000) The neural basis of romantic love. *Neuroreport* 11, 3829-3834.

Bartels A, Zeki S. (2004) The neural correlates of maternal and romantic love. Neuroimage 21, 1155-1166.

Barzun, J. *Darwin, Marx and Wagner; Critique of a Heritage.* New York, Garden City, 1950.

Beloff, Lord. Letter to *The Times*, July 5th, 1993.

Benedict, R. *Patterns of Culture.* New York, 1946.

Berkeley, G. *Three dialogues between Hylas and Philonus.* La Salle, Illinois, Open Court Publishing Company, 1954.

Borg J, Andree B, Soderstrom H, Farde L. (2003) The serotonin system and spiritual experiences. *Am. J.Psychiatry* 160,1965-1969.

Brain, WR. (1951) Mind and Matter. *Lancet* I, 863-867.

Brain, WR. (1955) Review of JF Delafresnaye (ed.) *Brain Mechanisms and Consciousness.* in *Brain*, 78, 669-671.

Brain, WR. (1963) Some reflections on brain and mind. *Brain*, 86, 381-402.

Britton WB, Bootzin RR. (2004) Near-death experiences and the temporal lobe. Psychol Sci. 15, 254-258.

Broad, CD. *Scientific Thought*. London, Routledge & Kegan Paul, 1923.

Brorson JR, Brewer K. (1988) St Paul and temporal lobe epilepsy. *J.Neurol.Neurosurg.Psychiatry* 51, 886-887.

Brown, JW. *Self and Process*. New York, Springer-Verlag, 1991.

Bucke RM. (1991) *Cosmic Consciousness*. London, Penguin.

Bullard, E. Preface to *The Great Ocean Business*. (B. Horsfield & PB Stone, eds.) London, Hodder & Stoughton, 1972.

Bullock, TH. *How do Brains Work? Papers of a Comparative Neurophysiologist*. Boston, Birkhauser, 1993.

Burtt, EA. *The Metaphysical Foundations of Science*. London, Routledge & Kegan Paul, 1932.

Byrd, RE. *Alone*. London, Putnam, 1939.

Carter CS. (1998) Neuroendocrine perspectives on social attachment and love. *Psychoneuroendocrinology* 23, 779-818.

Churchland, PM. *The Engine of Reason. The Seat of the Soul*. Cambridge, Mass. MIT Press, 1995.

Comfort, A. (1985) On physics and biology: getting their act together. *Perspect.Biol.Med.* 29, 1-9.

Comfort, A. (1989) A bridge to twenty-first century science. *Lancet* II, 1512-1513.

Crick, F. *The Astonishing Hypothesis*. New York, Scribner, 1994.

Crick, F and Koch, C. (1992) The problem of consciousness. *Sci. Amer.*, 267, pp. 110-117.

de Broglie, L. A general survey of the scientific work of Albert Einstein. in *Albert Einstein Philosopher-Scientist*. (P.A. Schlipp, ed.) New York, Harper & Row, 1959, pp 107-128.

Dent, NJH. *Rousseau*. Oxford, Blackwell, 1988.

Eccles, J. *The Neurophysiological Basis of Mind*. Oxford University Press, 1953.

Edelman, G. *Bright Air, Brilliant Fire*. London, Penguin, 1992.

Einstein, A. (1961) *Relativity. The Special and the General Theory.* (New York: Bonanza Books, p. 150).

Einstein, A, Bergmann, P (1938) On a generalization of Kaluza's theory of electricity. *Ann. Math.* 39, 683-701.

Ellis, R. *An Ontology of Consciousness.* Dordrecht, Kluwer, 1986.

Esch T, Stefano GB. (2005) The neurobiology of love. *Neur. Endocrinol.Lett.* 26, 175-192.

Esposito, J.L. *Islam. The Straight Path.* Oxford University Press. 1998.

Fischer H, Aron A, Brown LL. (2005) Romantic love: an fMRI study of a neural mechanism for mate choice. *J.Comp.Neurol.* 493, 58-62.

Fitzgerald, BD and Berman, D. (1994) Of sound mind. *Nature* 368, 92.

Foster, J. *The Immaterial Self: a Defence of the Cartesian Dualist Conception of Mind.* London, Routledge, 1990.

Frankl, V. The primacy of the abstract. in *Beyond Reductionism* (A. Koestler & J Smythies eds.) Boston, Beacon Press, 1973a.

Frankl, V. *The Doctor and the Soul.* New York, Random House, 1973b.

Freeman, D. *Margaret Mead and Samoa: the Making and Unmaking of an Anthropological Myth.* Cambridge, Mass. Harvard University Press, 1983.

Freeman, DZ and van Nieuwenhuizen P. (1985) The hidden dimensions of space-time. *Sci.Amer.,* 252, 74-81.

Freemon FR. (1976) A differential diagnosis of the inspirational spells of Muhammad the Prophet of Islam. *Epilepsia,* 17, 423-427.

Gray, J. (1992) Consciousness on the scientific agenda. *Nature,* 358, 277.

Heidegger M. The way back into the ground of metaphysics. In *Existentialism from Dostoevesky to Sartre* (W A Kaufman, ed.) New York, Meridan Books, 1958, p. 215.

Heidegger, M. *Being and Time* (tr. J. Macquerie & E. Robinson). New York, Harper & Row, 1962.

Heywood, R. *Beyond the Reach of Sense: an Enquiry into Extrasensory Perception.* New York, Dutton, 1961.

Hinton, CH. *The Fourth Dimension.* London, Swan Sonnenschein, 1906.

Honderich, T. *A Theory of Determinism: the Mind, Neuroscience and Life Hopes.* Oxford, Clarendon Press, 1988.

Huxley, A. *The Perennial Philosophy.* London. Chatto and Windus.

Huxley, A. *Heaven and Hell.* London, Chatto & Windus, 1956.

Huxley, J. *Religion without Revelation.* New York, Mentor, p. 19.

James W. (2004) *The Varieties of Religious Experience.* New York, Simon & Schuster.

Jeans, Sir James. *The Mysterious Universe.* Cambridge University Press, 1930.

Johnson, P. *Intellectuals.* London, Harper & Row, 1988.

Johnson RC. (1953) *The Imprisioned Splendour.* London. Hodder & Stoughton.

Jung, CG. *The Structure and Dynamics of the Psyche.* New York, Pantheon books, 1960.

Jung, CG. Personal communication, 1952.

Kaluza, P. On the unity problem in physics. In T. Appelquist, A. Chodos, PGO Freund (eds.) *Modern Kaluza-Klein Theories.* Menlo Park, Addison-Wesley, 1987.

Kendrick KM. (2004) The neurobiology of social bonds. *J. Neuroendocrinol.* 16, 1007-1008.

Kosslyn, S. *Image and mind.* Cambridge, Mass. Harvard University Press, 1980.

Kurup RK, Kurup PA. (2003) Hypothalamic digoxin, hemispheric dominance, and neurobiology of love and affection. *Int.J.Neurosci.* 113, 721-729.

Landsborough D.(1987) St. Paul and temporal lobe epilepsy. *J Neurol Neurosurg Psychiat.* 50, 659-664.

Lewis, D. *On the Plurality of Worlds.* Oxford, Blackwell, 1986.

Linde, A. *Particle Physics and Inflationary Cosmology.* Chur, Harwood Academic Publishers, 1990.

Machiavelli, N. *The Discourses.* Translation by L.J. Walker. Edited by Bernard Crick. Penguin 1970.

Madell, G. *Mind and Materialism.* Edinburgh University Press, 1988.

Markosian, N. (1992) On language and the passage of time. *Phil. Studies,* 66, 1-26

Marshall, J.C. (1991) Unscientific postscript. *Nature,* 347, 435.

Mead, M. *Coming of Age in Samoa.* New York, Morrow, 1928.

Mijuskovic, B. (1978) Brentano's theory of consciousness. *Phil. Phenomenol.Res,.* 38, 315-324.

Moody, R. *Life after Life: An Investigation of a Phenomenon-Survival of Bodily Death.* 1976. New York, Bantam Press, 1976.

Myers, F. *Human Personality and its Survival of Bodily Death.* New York, Longmans Green, 1954.

Nagel, T. What is the mind-brain problem? In *Experimental and Theoretical Studies of Consciousness.* CIBA Foundation Symposium 174. GR Bock & J Marsh (eds). New York, Wiley, 1993.

Najib A, Lorberbaum JP, Kose S, Bohning DE, George MS. (2004) Regional brain activity in women grieving a romantic relationship breakup. *Am.J. Psychiatry,* 161, 2245-2256.

O'Brien, R. (1989) Viewpoint. Is rock the worst music ever written? *The Daily Telegraph,* November 8th.

Ozkara C, Sary H, Hanoglu L, Yeni N, Avdogdu I, Ozyurt E. (2004) Icta kissing and religious speech in a patient with right temporal lobe epilepsy. *Epileptoc Disord.* 6, 241-245.

Page, IH. (1957) Chemistry of the brain; past perfect, present indicative and future perfect. *Science,* 125, 721-727.

Penrose, R. *The Emperor's New Mind.* Oxford University Press, 1989.

Penrose, R. *Shadows of the Mind: a search for the missing science of consciousness.* Oxford University Press, 1994.

Persinger MA. (1983) Religious and mystical experiences as artifacts of temporal lobe function: a general hypothesis. *Percept.Mot.Skills* 57, 1255-1262.

Pippard, B. (1992) Review of B. Appleyard *Understanding Present Science and the Soul of Modern Man. Nature*, 357, 29.

Popper, K. *The Open Society and its Enemies.* London, Routledge & Kegan Paul, 1962.

Porter, G. (1975) Letter to *The Times*, June 21st.

Previc FH. (2006) The role of the extrapersonal brain systems in eligious activity. *Cnosioos Cogn.* Jan. 23 Epub.

Price, HH. Survival and the idea of another world. in *Brain and Mind* (J.R. Smythies ed.) London, Routledge & Kegan Paul, 1965.

Puccetti, R. in *The Case for Dualism.* (J. Smythies & J. Beloff, eds.). Charlottesville, University Press of Virginia, 1989.

Quartz, SR and Sejnowski TJ. (1997) The neural basis of cognitive development: a constructionist manifesto. *Behav. Brain Sci. 20, 537-556.*

Ramachandran VS and Blakeslee S. (1998) *Phantoms in the Brain.* New York, Morrow.

Rees-Mogg, W. (1990) Rough justice from a phoney intelligensia. *The Independent*, June 4th.

Reichenbach, H. *The Philosophy of Space and Time.* New York, Dover, 1958.

Reichenbach, H. *The Direction of Time.* (M. Reichenbach, ed.) Berkeley, University of California Press, 1971.

Rescher, N. (1990) Postmodernity and paranoia. *Amer.Phil. Quart.,* 27, 89-99.

Richardson, RC. (1982) The "scandal" of Cartesian interactionism. *Mind,* 81, 20-37.

Rorty, R. *Contingency, Irony and Solidarity*. Cambridge University Press, 1989.

Rousseau, J-J. Discourses on the arts and sciences. in *The Social Contract* (tr. G.D.H. Cole). London, Dent, 1973.

Russell, B. *Human Knowledge. Its Scope and Limits.* London, Allen & Unwin, 1948.

Russell, B. *The Autobiography of Bertrand Russell.* London, Allen & Unwin, 1967.

Ryle, G. (1924) from a letter to J. King Gordon quoted by J. Westphal and C. Chenn (1990) Is life absurd? *Philosophy*, 65, 199-203.

Sartre, J-P. *Existentialism and Human Emotions.* (Tr. B. Frechtme). New York, Philosophical Library, 1957.

Schrödinger, E. *Mind and Matter.* Cambridge University Press, 1958.

Sharpe, RA. (1980) review of PM Churchland *Scientific Realism and the Plasticity of Mind.* In *Phil.Quart.*, 30, 268-269.

Shermer, M. (2006) The political brain. *Sci.Amer.* 295, 36.

Sirag, S-P. *Plato's Cave Revisited: the Projection of Space-Time from C[S4]..* unpublished ms.

Smythies, JR. (1954) Analysis of projection. *Brit J Phil Sci.*, 5, 120-158.

Smythies, JR. (1959a) The stroboscopic patterns. Part I. The dark phase. *Brit.J Psychol.*, 50,106.

Smythies, JR. (1959b) The stroboscopic patterns. Part II. The phenomenology of the bright phase and after-images. *Brit J Psychol.*, 50, 305.

Smythies, JR. (1960) The stroboscopic patterns. Part III. Further experiments and discussion. *Brit J Psychol..* 51, 247.

Smythies, JR *The Walls of Plato's Cave.* Aldershot, Avebury, 1994a.

Smythies, JR. On the nature of consciousness and the unconscious from the point of view of neuroscience and neurophilosophy. in *The Neurological Boundaries of Reality.* Critchley (ed.) London, Farrand Books, 1994b.

Smythies, JR. (1994c) Requiem for the Identity Theory. *Inquiry*, 37, 311-329.

Smythies, JR. (1996) A note on the concept of the visual field in neurology, psychology, and visual neuroscience. *Perception*, 25; 369-371.

Smythies, JR. (1997) The biochemical basis of synaptic plasticity and neurocomputation: a new theory. *Proc.Roy.Soc. London B.*, 264, 575-579.

Smythies, J. (2003) Space, Time and Consciousness. *J. Consciousness Studies.* 10, 47-56

Smythies, JR and Ramachandran, VS. (1998) An empirical refutation of the Direct Realist theory of perception. *Inquiry*, 40, 437-438.

Squires, EJ. (1991) One mind or many— a note on the Everett interpretation of quantum theory. *Synthese*, 89, 283-286.

Stannard, R. (1987) Making sense of God's time. *The Times* August 22nd.

Stent, GS. (1987) The mind-brain problem. *Science*, 236, 990-992.

Stevenson, I. *Where Reincarnation and Biology Intersect.* Westport, Praeger, 1997.

Stewertka, SA. (1993) The stroboscopic patterns as dissipative structures. *Neurosci.Biobehav.Rev.*, 17, 69-78.

Stroll, A. *Sketches of Landscapes.* Cambridge, MA., MIT Press. 1998

Stroll, A. *Did my genes make me do it?* New York, Oneworld Publishing, 2006.

Tucker DM, Novelly RA, Walker PJ. (1987) Hyperreliogiosity in temporal lobe epilepsy: redefining the relationship. *J.Nerv.Ment.Dis.* 175, 181-184.

Tyrrell GNM. (1946) *The Personality of Man.* London, Pelican

Uus, U. *The Blindness of Modern Science.* Tartu, Tartu Observatory Press.

van Slooten, ER. (1986) Poe's Universes. *Nature,* 323, 198.

Vivas, E. *Contra Marcuse.* New Rochelle, Arlington House, 1971.

Walshe, FMR. (1951) Review of JZ Young. *Doubt and Certainty in Science. Brain,* 74, 522-523.

Walshe, FMR. (1953) Thoughts on the equation of mind with brain. *Brain,* 96, 1-18.

Williams, C. *All Hallows Eve.* London, Faber, 1946.

Wuerfel J, Krishnamoorthy ES, Brown RJ, Lemieux L, Koepp M, Tebartz van Elst I, Trimble MR. (2004) Religiosity is associated with hippocampal but not amygdala volumes in patients with refractory epilepsy. *J.Neurol.Neurosurg.Psychiatry* 75, 640-842.

Yahya, H. (2002) *Tell me about Creation*. New Delhi, Goodword

Zemach, E.M . (1986) Truth and beauty. *Phil. Forum,* 18, 21-39.

Zimerman, ME. (1989) The thorn in Heidegger's side: the question of National Socialism." *Phil. Forum,* 20, 326-365.

APPENDIX

Correspondence with H.H. Price and C.D. Broad.

Letters from Professor H. H. Price to John Smythies.

I first met Henry Habberley Price in London in 1950 as fellow members of the SPR. Shortly afterwards he was one of our subjects in the experiments we were carrying out at that time on the psychological effects of mescaline as part of our researches into the possible biochemical basis of schizophrenia. Thereafter we remained in frequent contact and became close friends. He was at all times the most considerate, courteous and helpful of mentors and possessed a gentle character and warm personality that reflected older and more worthy values than those most of the world lives by today.

Letter 1.
New College
Oxford
June 30th 1951

Dear Dr. Smythies,

Thank you very much for your letter and for the paper on Mescaline Phenomena[36] which interested me greatly. In fact it interested me so much that I am determined to try taking mescaline myself. Would you be willing to administer some to me sometime? It seems to me that philosophers and psychical researchers (and a fortiori people who are both at once) might have to have these very remarkable experiences for themselves, at first hand. The changes in the appearance of familiar environmental objects are as interesting, perhaps, as the purely visionary sense-data are, though the purely visionary ones would be more exciting. The synaesthetic experiences are very odd too — and certainly like some of the things on reads in mediumistic communications. And finally, I notice one of the subjects had an experience apparently resembling the Buddhist Nirvana (px, line 3).

I suppose one would need to give up 24 hours or more to the experiment — allowing for the after-effects — but it would be very worth while, and I really should very much like to try it, preferably under your supervision, or else under someone else's whom you can recommend.

I am interested in what you have to say about the amputated limb illusion, because I have just been writing a contribution to a discussion on 'Seeming' for a philosophical gathering in July. It is, I think, important to distinguish between (intellectual) 'seeming' and (sensory) 'appearing'. Philosophers have an almost irresistible inclination nowadays to identify them. I have already remarked in the paper I have written that they would not do this if they had ever been delirious.

yours sincerely

H.H. Price.

Letter 2 (extract).
New College
Oxford
Feb.9th 1952

Thank you too for the copy of your letter to Mr. Flew. Your comments on the difficulty of 'getting the hang' of contemporary philosophy arouses my heartfelt sympathy. But I hope that will not give up the use of the word 'mind' altogether. It is a dangerous word, no doubt (what word is not?) but I think the dangers of a purely Behaviourist theory of human personality are even greater.

Letter 3 (extract)
June 16, 1952

Philosophy, especially in the present phase of its development, does have to be learned largely by means of the spoken word, and especially by oral discussions among small groups of people. It was so in Socrates' time, and it is so still. Of course one must read books too (some people don't do it enough) and not least the philosophical classics from Descartes onwards, which do not get out of date with the lapse of time as scientific books do. But reading by itself, however careful, will not give one everything that is needed.

If you want a very good statement of the way in which many present day British philosophers approach these problems, let me recommend the article on the first two pages of the current <u>Times Literary Supplement</u>. It is by a very able Oxford colleague of mine, S. N. Hampshire of this College. I don't altogether agree with the approach myself—the emphasis on 'ordinary language' seems to me somewhat sterilizing and cramping (you may have noticed it in Flew's comments on your article[37] in the *Journal*). But whether one likes it or not, this way of conceiving philosophical problems does have to be reckoned with, if one wants to get a hearing for one's views; and one can only learn about it by having oral discussions with its exponents—not just by reading.

I have been trying to write a review for <u>Mind</u> of a book called 'The Perception of the Visual World' by an American psychologist, James J. Gibson (published in this country by Allen & Unwin). Probably you have read it already, but if not, I hope you will. I cannot judge many of the technical details, but he does seem to me a very intelligent and original man.

yours sincerely

H.H.Price

Letter 4
New College
Oxford
July 17th 1952

Dear Dr. Smythies,

This is just a line to thank you, and your wife too, for your kind hospitality (I am sure I was a most inconvenient guest) and still more for giving me one of the most agreeable and interesting experiences I have ever had. I wish that all my philosophical colleagues would try mescaline, and I shall try and persuade some of them to do so. One of their besetting sins is that they tend to be too sane, normal and common-sensical. I have told Professor Hornell Hart that he should try it too, if only because of his interest in what he calls 'clear dreams'. My feeling about the experience is that the drug does not so much 'induce' anything, but rather just 'releases' certain perceptual capacities which were there all the time. And it would not surprise me if they were 'releasable' in other ways as well e.g. by means of Yogic practices. However this may be, I would not have missed the experience for anything, and I am much indebted to you for your kindness and also for your professional skill.

My very best wishes to your wife and yourself for a very pleasant holiday, and again many thanks to you both—and to Mr. Osborn too.

yours sincerely

H.H. Price

Letter 5. This letter comments on the prepublication correspondence between Dr. Smythies and Sir Francis Walshe, Editor of *Brain*, concerning Dr. Smythies' paper "The experience and description of the human body" subsequently published in *Brain,* Vol. 76; p. 132. 1953.

Hillside
Headington Hill
Oxford
August 22nd, 1952

Dear Dr. Smythies,

Thank you very much for this paper and the attached correspondence, also for your letter. Unfortunately, I <u>am</u> rather busy at the moment writing a whole course of new lectures for next term, and not getting on so fast as I could wish, either. But I will make a few brief comments all the same, for what they may be worth.

Certainly I agree with you that Physiological Idealism and Naive Realism cannot both be true. I can imagine someone saying that there is some truth in each of them, and that a satisfactory theory must do justice to the 'element of truth' there is in both etc: & that is as far as I would be willing to go. It may be that Dr. Walshe, as a disciple of Whitehead, is influenced by the coherence theory of truth, according to which there are degrees of truth and no proposition whatever is wholly false (this is the theory of the Hegelian Absolute Idealist school, by which Whitehead was somewhat influenced).

But I cannot help suspecting, also, that Dr. Walshe has not distinguished clearly between <u>Realism</u> and <u>Naive Realism</u>. c.f.

his marginal notes on p. viii. What you have said about Sirius etc. is certainly the language of Realism—i.e. a theory which says that there is a world of physical objects independent of our minds—but it does not follow that this is the language of *Naive* Realism as he seems to think. Naive Realism is only one variety of Realism, and not a very plausible one. I think it would help if you made this point yourself.

But there is something else to be said about Naive Realism, which you havent said, and which might perhaps help to placate Dr. Walshe. Throughout, you emphasize the <u>defects</u> of Naive Realism. But it has its points too. The Naive Realist attitude of 'common sense' surely has very great biological utility. The ordinary man—or animal—could hardly have lived without it. In all men who havent been able to replace it by the more sophisticated Realism of science—and even in those in their ordinary unscientific activities, e.g. eating, driving a car,—it could be said that a Naive Realist attitude is one of the essential constituents of sanity. Speaking rather anthromorphically, it could be said that the Naive Realist attitude is one of Nature's most ingenious and successful devices. Like all her devices, it is not 100 per cent successful (there are occasionally illusions and hallucinations) but it still works very well in <u>nearly</u> all the situation which the ordinary manor animal encounters. Whereas mere inspection of sensa, <u>without</u> taking them to be identical with the surfaces of material objects, would not enable him to survive a day. The Naive Realist attitude then is not just a nuisance, which we must get rid of as soon as we can. It is comparable rather to an organ, and one so useful that we can hardly survive without it; if we are to get rid of it (to the extent that we can) we must replace it by something which will do the same job better—and that will have to be the more sophisticated and "critical" Realism, which is in fact the foundation of science. It is not the Realism which is wrong, it is the naiveté, the simplifying and biologically-useful assumption that the relation between sensa and material objects is nothing more complicated than the relation of 'being identical with parts of the surface of...' or something of the sort. The problem is to define this relation in a more complicated way which will do justice to <u>all</u> the relevant facts; including the highly relevant fact that somehow or other, by means of sensing sensa, we manage to get knowledge of the physical world, and of our own physical organisms as a part of it. This, I suggest, is the right way to look at Naive Realism. It is mistaken, yes: but not completely and utterly mistaken. Its mistake is a mistake of over-simplification. And it is better to be a Naive Realist than not to be a Realist at all—i.e. to deny that there is a physical world, a spatio-temporal world of some kind independent of our minds, or to deny that we can know anything about it.

I think that you have not done justice to the merits of naive Realism, as well as the defects, and therefore may have given the impression to Dr. Walshe that you reject realism altogether and have deprived yourself of the right to use <u>any</u> sort of realistic language. The curious remark in his letter 'you seem to say that experience is not true but that abstractions derived from it are true' suggests that he does think that you are rejecting realism altogether, as does the marginal note on p viii which I have mentioned already. See also para. 3 of his letter. "lapsing into the language of naive realism" when he <u>should</u> have said "of Realism". I agree that it doesn't really make sense to call experiences either true or false. But I think one could paraphrase his remark thus 'you think that experience gives us no knowledge (or justifiable beliefs) about anything but sensa; but in fact it does—somehow—give us knowledge about physical objects; though not in the way the <u>Naive</u> realist says it does." This is in fact the criticism which Whitehead makes of Hume in a little book called <u>Symbolism and Truth</u>—a very obscure and most annoying little book, but very well worth reading all the same.

There is however another criticism in Dr. Walshe's letter, p.2 para 3 and 4, which I cannot see how to whitewash even partially. Why should he think that there is any inconsistency at all between saying (a) physical objects are <u>not</u> directly inspectable and (b) other entities, viz. sensa & sense-fields, <u>are</u> directly inspectable? The fact that we cannot inspect X does not deprive us of the power of inspecting something else Y which is entirely different from X. Perhaps however you should have made this clear that 'stroboscopic patterns" means 'certain directly experienced <u>sensory</u> patterns'. If he should then complain that you have no right to use the word 'stroboscopic' (on the ground that it is a physical-object word) this is the same confusion as I have noted before between Naive Realist language and Realist language as such.

It seems to me that the distinction you have drawn between the Perceived Body, the Body-Image, the Body-Schema, and the Body-Concept—the main point of the paper—are very proper and necessary distinctions, especially if people have the unfortunate habit of using the term 'body-image' for all four. At any rate what you say on the subject appears clear and convincing to an outsider like me who hasn't read the literature.

Just two minor point in conclusion about Schilder, whom I havent read. First, what did he mean by "perhaps the body itself is a phantom" (Quoted on p. xiii) A strange and tantalizing remark! Secondly, as to the word 'representation' (passage quoted on p xix). If the word was <u>vorstellung</u> this is commonly used by Germans as the equivalent of the English word 'idea'—in Locke's very wide and vague use of the term 'idea', covering images as well as concepts. So 'not a mere representation' (nicht blosse Vorstellung?) would most probably mean 'not a mere mental image'. You however have interpreted 'mere representation' to mean what an ordinary English writer would mean by it.

I admit however that some German <u>philosophers</u>, notably Kant. have used the word vorstellung to cover sensa as well (as 'idea' sometimes does in Locke) in which case a careful translator would render it 'presentation' or 'sense presentation'. But I dont think this is the way a physiologist or psychologist would be likely to use it. He has the word <u>empfindung</u> for that. But I am no expert in the German tongue, far from it! It is indeed a terrible language, and if one wants to be obscure and ambiguous, it offers one endless opportunities.

These are all the remarks that occur to me, and I fear that they are not very helpful. And I have an uneasy conscience anyway, because I should have written before to thank you for sending me another paper (about Professor Hart), but have been too distracted with lecture-writing to be able to think about it.

My very best wishes to your wife and yourself. I hope that you had a very happy time in Ireland.

yours sincerely

H.H. Price.

Letter 6.
New College
Oxford
Aug. 26th 1952

Dear Dr. Smythies,
Thank you very much for your letter. This is just a line to say that of course you are most welcome to quote anything you like from my previous letter.

As for 'Physiological Idealism', I agree that it is a misleading phrase. But perhaps the reason it is used is this — that certain sense-given properties such as red, hot, hard (in the <u>sensory</u> sense of the words, not the physicist's sense) are thought to be created by processes in the brain and to have no existence apart from these processes: and the same applies to sensible <u>Gestalt</u>-qualities too, e.g. visible shape. The theory is 'idealistic' in the sense that it holds these qualities to be 'subjective' (i.e. brain-dependent) — and not 'objective': as the naive Realist supposes them to be.

This is the classical problem of the status of so-called 'secondary qualities'. The terminology of primary and secondary qualities was introduced by Locke, and the chapter about it in his <u>Essay Concerning Human Understanding</u> is still very well worth reading, if only because of the influence it has had on determining the outlook of scientists ever since. It is Ch. 8 of Book II of the <u>Essays</u> and it is rather misleadingly entitled 'Some further considerations concerning our simple ideas.' Locke himself was a medical man, as well as a philosopher, and was in close touch with the physicists and physiologists of the time (1690)—the epoch in which all this trouble started.

yours sincerely

H.H. Price

Letter 7.
New College
Oxford
Dec. 3rd 1952

Dear Dr. Smythies,

Thank you very much for your letter. I have written to Professor Le Gros Clark, and hope my note to him will do good rather than harm! He is reputed to be rather a formidable man (I hardly know him myself) and moreover is said, truly or falsely, to have Marxist or semi-Marxist inclinations. I naturally had to say that you are interested in the relations between Neurology and the Epistemology of sense perception; I added that I took your views on the subject seriously, and that I thought my philosophical colleagues here would do the same. But he very likely thinks that there isn't such a subject as Epistemology, or ought not to be if there is. And then my remarks will have done you harm rather than good. Naturally, I took care to say nothing at all about Psychical Research.

I am very glad that your research is going well. As a matter of fact, Osborn [then Editor of the SPR Journal] was telling me something about it only two nights ago, and it sounded most exciting. I went to London to hear my mescaline record played over (so that we could decide how much of it should be typed out for future reference) and we had dinner with Mrs. Heywood [author of "The Sixth Sense"]. Her records were played too, and I listened to them with great interest and some amazement! Her semi-mystical experiences were most curious. It sounded as if she had been inspecting Platonic Archetypes and I almost began to wonder whether Socrates and Plato could have been mescal addicts. Her strong emotional reactions when the letters were put into her hands was also very odd. She does have some mediumistic power, I think, so perhaps a little genuine clairvoyance occurred at that point; but the chief thing seems to have been that she so much disliked being brought back again from the heights, or depths, into contact with this rather sordid and all-too-human world—and this, I think, is very frequent with mystical people in all ages and countries.

I found that I had forgotten quite a number of my own experiences, especially the eye-shut ones, but not the most exciting one, which was the aesthetic transformation of quite common place visible objects. This is one of the most delightful and interesting experiences I have ever had. When I was in the Lake District later in the summer the mountains at the head of Borrowdale for a very short time (five minutes perhaps) looked as your chair and the street outside had looked—much the same curious 'enriching' of their colours, though in a much smaller degree. I went back to the house to fetch my painting apparatus, but of course it was too late! They were just ordinary mountains again—very nice ones, no doubt, but nothing more.

I hope that your wife and yourself are in the best of health, despite 40 degrees of frost, and that you are both having a very nice time. I hear a rumour that an addition to the family is expected before very long. I hope that this is true, and that all will go very well.

Best wishes to you both for Christmas and the New Year.
yours sincerely

H.H.Price.

p.s. If you come to Oxford next year, I hope that will dose all the Oxford philosophers with mescaline, and especially the more common-sensical ones.

Letter 8. Comments on my paper 'Analysis of projection' published in *Brit.J.Phil.Sci.* 5, 120, 1954
New College
Oxford

April 12th, 1953

Dear Smythies

Thank you very much for this paper. I have been rather lazy about it I am afraid, being preoccupied with writing some lectures for next term. But I have now at last read it, and have very much enjoyed it too. I have made a number of notes and suggestions in pencil on the margins of the typescript itself. (I hope you do not mind; they can easily be rubbed out). Nearly all of them are concerned with points of style and exposition. My own experience of writing papers suggests that such apparently minor points are really quite important. If I am not mistaken, there is a great deal in this paper—not only the main thesis, but many of the details as well—which will be completely unfamiliar to the majority of your readers. It is extraordinary how the most intelligent readers can misunderstand things which are perfectly clear to oneself! It is worth while taking some trouble to remove even the very small obscurities and ambiguities.

I will now mention a few points that have occurred to me:—

p. ii. Is a <u>black</u> sensum a good example. It seems to me to introduce an unnecessary difficulty. Don't physiologists say that black is "not a positive sensation"?[38] A <u>green</u> sensum would do as well for your purposes.

p. ii med. (projection) "back to their <u>extra-somatic</u> place of origin" would make it quite clear.

p. iii. med. An unreadable sentence with too many "whiches". Instead of "by this movement and which..." you could say "by this movement. And yet these cortical patterns form the neuronal basis for..."

p. iii <u>Res cogitans</u> (should be italicised). Add that in Descartes terminology this doesnt just mean the "<u>thinking</u> thing"—the traditional translation—but rather the "conscious thing". He uses the word <u>cogitans</u> in a very wide way.

p. v .5/8 'self-directed'. Ambiguous—might mean 'autonomous'. Avoid the ambiguity by writing <u>S</u>elf-directed, with capital S, as in p. viii below.

p. v. fin. "of the former, the perceived body'. Ambiguous. Actually 'the former' is the <u>physical body</u>. Add in brackets "(This model is the <u>perceived</u> body, the somatic sensory field.)"

p. vi. fin. Obscure sentence. I suggest "These ψγ and ψκ mechanisms are as much part of the total organism as are the ordinary sensory fields themselves."

Few of your readers, if any, will have read T. and W.'s [Thouless and Wiesner] paper. Should the letters γ and κ be explained to them? (γ is the first letter of the Greek word γιγνωεκητ 'to know, and κ of the word κινην 'to move'). I tremble to suggest it, but will all of them know that the Greek letter ψ is read 'Psi'? It is called psi below on p. ix. Will all of them know that this is the same as ψ?

p. vii. "Relation between perceptual space and physical space". This—as ordinarily discussed—is not <u>just</u> a relation between sensory fields and the physical organism; but also (and more typically) a relation between sensory fields and <u>extra-somatic objects</u>. If for example the relation between the apparent movement of the landscape (when one is travelling in a train) and its physical fixity, or again double vision etc. or any of the phenomena of perspective. These are the sorts of instances which Broad has in mind in the passage quoted below.

p. vii The Self is apparently <u>not</u> the last term of the ψγchain, whereas it is the first term of the ψγ one. Is that right?

p. viii "structurally <u>independent</u> of the brain structure'. This might suggest that there is no <u>causal</u> relationship between brain-events and sensa. Could one say 'and that their spatial structure is <u>geometrically different from</u> the spatial structure of the brain' or 'they have a different geometry from brain processes.'?

p. ix. l. 1 Can 'psi-fields' be right/ Psi-<u>mechanisms</u>? (As a matter of fact, only one of them—the ψγ one—seems to be relevant here). Add a footnote referring back to p. vi for your readers, as I have remarked already, will be totally unfamiliar with this ψ terminology.

p. ix 3/4 'coordinates all imagery'. But images are part of the psyche itself, as sensa are. What the brain co-ordinates, then, must be the cerebral memory traces or the like—the cerebral correlates of images, not the images themselves.

p. ix 5/6 sub-par (9) This is the first we have heard of the autonomous activity of the psyche, though we could guess that the autonomous activity of the Self initiates ψγ processes. The fact that the psyche does have autonomous activities, and the fact that it is biologically useful that they should be inhibited, is enormously important, and shouldnt be introduced in this abrupt way without any preparation. If you think, as I believe you do, that the production of sensa themselves is one of the psyche's autonomous activities, this should have been made clear much earlier.

By the way, I should have said earlier that the distinction you draw between the Psyche and the Self also needs further explanation. It is not too familiar to the majority of students of philosophy (though it is of course a commonplace of the classical Hindu philosophy, which they don't read) still less will it be familiar to neurologists. Note also that Descartes drew no such distinction—he being the one philosopher whose views neurologists have some acquaintance with.

p. (xi) This page ends abruptly. Is there a further page that is missing from this copy? It is odd to polish off 'unconscious mind' in a mere seven lines!

These are the main points that I wanted to mention. There are a few other small ones which you will find indicated in pencil, in the margins of the text.

I ought to have written long ago to thank you for your criticism of my lecture on 'Survival and the idea of another world'. They are going to appear in the forthcoming number of the SPR Journal and I hope to make a reply of some kind in the next number—if I can think of any reply!

I hope that your research is going well, and that you will soon be back in this country. My very best wishes to your wife and yourself.

yours sincerely

H.H. Price

p.s. It is very good news that Aldous Huxley is going to try mescal. He is just the man who ought to[39]

Letter 9. Written in response to an enquiry as to suitable subjects amongst philosophers for possible future mescaline experiments[40].

New College
Oxford
July 20th 1953

Dear Dr. Smythies,
Thank you very much for your two large envelopes and their contents, which only reached me yesterday evening, on my return from a fortnight in Ireland. I cannot do anything about your examination of HHP's Philosophy for a fortnight or so, because I have to finish writing an Eddington Memorial Lecture (on Science, Religion and Psychical Research) which has to be sent to the Cambridge University Press a long time beforehand, and then I have to attend an International Parapsychology Congress at Utrecht. But I shall be very glad to read the paper, if you dont mind waiting and will send you any comments that occur to me. I must however write at once to tell you how interested I am in the project you are submitting to the Ford Foundation, and I shall be very glad indeed to be an Advisor along with Aldous Huxley. As to the questions you ask me, Professor C. J. Ducasse should certainly be approached, and also Professor W.T. Stace of Princeton, who is greatly interested in mystical experience. I dont know of any likely philosopher in Canada, or in Latin America. In this country you should certainly try Prof. Ryle and Prof. Ayer and perhaps also my colleague William Kurald [?] of Exeter College, Oxford. In Cambridge, both Professor John Wisdom (Trinity) and Professor R. B. Braithwaite (King's) should certainly be approached, and so should Professor Broad, who has just retired from his chair. It so happens that Broad is to be at Ann Arbor, Michigan, for the coming autumn term and is then going to California in Dec.

or January. The difficulty is (this is strictly between ourselves) that he is unusually susceptible to nausea & vomiting and he would need special reassurance on that point. Adrian gave him some mescal a long time ago. The only result was to make him very sick, and he had to take an antidote. Once this difficulty is overcome — In France there are two philosophers whom you might think of. Professor Marcel and Professor Morlau-Ponthy [?]. In Copenhagen, there is an influential philosopher called Jørgenson —a very intelligent person, but perhaps too much of a pure logician to be interested. He would be worth trying all the same. Is that enough to be going on with? I dare say I shall be able to think of some more later. My best regards to your wife and to the baby too. I am delighted to hear that all three of you are flourishing.

yours sincerely

H.H. Price

p.s. I think that in your statement to the Ford Foundation you have forgotten about the <u>Yoga</u> practices of the Far East. These (or some of them) are deliberate and systematic attempts to obtain mystical experiences.

Letter 10. The typescript referred to is an early draft of my book "Analysis of Perception" that was published in 1956 with a preface by Sir Russell Brain.

New College
Oxford
August 16th 1953

Dear Smythies,
Thank you for the new installment of typescripts, which arrived the day after I had sent back the previous one and some comments on it. I am afraid I cannot do anything about this new lot in the immediate future, because I am very busy with lectures just now, and as soon as they are finished I must read another typescript which an ex-pupil in America has sent me;

and I have promised to read still another one, not very long I hope, for someone else before the beginning of term. So in one way and another I am rather snowed under with typescripts at present; and you must please not mind if I keep you waiting for a while. Also I should warn you in good time that I have a very special horror of writing forewords and introductions! One has to do it is one is editing a posthumous work by someone else, and a very troublesome job it is too. I have just done it for the new edition of Tyrrell's "Apparitions', which is going to come out in book form shortly. But so far as writers in <u>this</u> world are concerned, my view is that they should introduce themselves. If it is felt that any introduction is needed; and I believe that is what the reader prefers too. If there is an introduction or preface by someone other than the main author, I think this is apt to make the reader suspicious, as if the book was being apologised for. Perhaps I am prejudiced about this, and if so you must please forgive my intemperate language.

However that may be, I look forward to reading your chapters; and may I add that I don't see any answer to the criticisms you make about the knobbly stone—unless it be that in <u>short</u>-range vision our experience of "visual depths" is adequate for the job (e.g. if the knobbly stone were, say, a yard away.) It is true that I did habitually use simple-shaped things like matchboxes as examples. But one reason for this was that we have no adjectives—or at least ungrammatical persons like myself have none—for describing complicated shapes in a manner intelligible to the reader.

Best wishes to all three of you, and I hope you are now getting a real Canadian summer.

yours sincerely

H.H. Price

Letter 11. Comment on an early draft of my book "*Analysis of Perception.*"
New College
Oxford

Sept. 21st, 1953

Dear Smythies,

Thank you very much for the typescript. I do apologise for being so slow about it. I had hoped to get it done while I was in Cumberland for the first fortnight of this month, but a lecture for the university of Aberdeen, which I had to finish first, took much longer than I expected, and I only got it done three days ago.

However, I have at last read this, and I haven't got any major criticisms to make. I have made a number of pencil notes in the margin (I hope you won't mind) and nearly all of them are concerned just with minor points of style and exposition. There are a few others as well which I will mention now.

1. Ch.II (Broad) p. 1 ad fi. "In this multi-dimensional space…" I am puzzled to know just what you are denying when you say "would not be one or other kind of section." Are you denying (a) Broad's (apparent) contention that the two kinds of space cannot be specifically described and distinguished from each other, whereas you yourself think they can? Or are you denying (b) his (apparent) contention that they are two <u>kinds</u> of space, and saying instead that they are merely two <u>sections</u> of one n-dimensional space.

2. Ch. III (s-datum genesis) p. 1, 2nd. sentence. Too complicated to be easily understood. Instead of "which could…" have a new sentence e.g. "no such system of knowledge, he says, could possibly be more certain than the knowledge obtained from an examination of sense-data themselves."

3. Ch. III p.12/3 Explain for the benefit of the lay reader what exactly the distinction between physiology and neurology is. Most people (including most philosophers) are by no means clear about the difference.

4. Ch.III, p.iv. fin. "effected largely through the sense of touch." Add a sentence or two to illustrate <u>how</u> it is effected. Some day by the way you should read Berkeley's Essay on the Theory of Vision. It looks as if some of his contentions have been confirmed by subsequent research (e.g. as to congenitally

blind people restored to sight). One of his main points of course is that the characteristics of the visual field are greatly influenced by tactual experience.

5. Ch.III, p. v med/ "may likewise be affected independently." Independently of what? I think you mean "independently of what is going on <u>in the retinal image</u> to which these sense-data or groups of sense-data belong." But this may not be clear to the reader, and should be specifically stated.

I think the empirical facts stated on pp iii et seq. of this chapter are of great interest.

6. Ch. V (Metaphys. Foundations of Neurology) p.2 is missing

7. Ch Iv last four lines. There is a kind of pun on the word 'material' here. 'Material' used as a noun has a wider meaning than 'material' used as an adjective. Used as a noun, it may mean <u>anything</u>, extended or unextended, out of which something is made. Used as an adjective, it applies only to extended entities, and normally to physical ones. By means of this play upon the word 'material' your paradox (for it is so one!) that the psyche is a material entity is made to seem less paradoxical than it is. Of course, though paradoxical, it may still be true.

8. Ch. V, p. 5. l.6. Here is the crucial distinction between the Psyche and the Observing Self ('Witness'). It should be emphasised more because most people are inclined to use the two terms as synonyms. There is a note about it at the foot of p 8 but I think something more should be said on p 5 as well. You are certain to be misunderstood unless you are very explicit on the point. It should also be made quite clear that you use 'Ego' as a synonym for 'Observing Self'—because 'ego' too is often used as an alternative term for 'Psyche' or 'Mind' etc.

I think it would be a good thing if you put in a table or diagram somewhere—a schematic map, as it were, of the 'total human organism'.

9. Ch.V p.8 (line 4 of Siii) ?insert (it seems to be called for) "And in any case the parietal lobe does not <u>perceive</u> at all." Scientists constantly write as though the brain—a material object— could perceive things, and as if it could think. I see you

do say below "the brain does not perceive space" but the point should be emphasized because many people are confused about it. It isnt merely that the brain does not perceive space, but that it does not <u>perceive</u> anything.

10. Ch. V p. 9 fin Location of consciousness. It has been said earlier that the Observing Self also has a location (p. 5 of this chapter, line 6) though I suppose it does not have any extension. Something could be said on this point here, especially in view of the almost universal tendency to confuse the observing self with the Psyche.

11. Ch. V. s vi p1. The second sentence is very long and involved. The reader will have to read it two or three times before he grasps it. Divide it into two, Also the concentration of three adverbs "always previously simply" is stylistically horrid. Try reading the sentence aloud and you will agree with me!

12. Ch.V svi p.1-p.2. This is very difficult for anyone who has not <u>already</u> understood your theory. It looks as if there were now <u>three</u> spaces (1) physical or public space (2) a whole lot of private spaces (3) what may be called 'psi-mechanism' space. Consequently it is not clear what is meant by 'these <u>two</u> space systems (p2 lines 4-5). One of them is evidently the psi-mechanism space. But which is the other? Also is psi-mechanism space <u>private</u> or not? I think it is not—unlike perceptual space

13. May I just add that this last section vi of Ch V seems to me to be much the most difficult part of the book? It is also one of the most important parts, and I think you should go through it carefully again and try to make it easier for the reader. If you leave it as it stands a lot of people will just get impatient with it and give it up in disgust or despair. I have made a lot of suggestions in pencil in the margins. You may not think much of them, but I hope they may at leas indicate the difficulties which the reader is likely to have over this section.

My very best wishes to your wife and to the infant and yourself, and I hope the research continues to go well.

yours sincerely

H.H. Price

p.s. Professor Broad should have arrived at Ann Arbor university, Michigan, by now. He is to be there until December, and is then going to California.

Letter 12
New College
Oxford
July 19th 1956

Dear Smythies,
It was very kind of you to send me a copy of your book[41], which has just arrived this morning. Thank you very much indeed. I have only just glanced inside it, but I can see that there are a lot of things in it which will interest me. I am very glad you have included a chapter on veridical and hallucinatory sense-experience, and I hope that philosophers will read it with care. They seldom seem to me to know anything about the empirical facts of hallucination and the only examples they ever discuss are pink rats and Macbeth's dagger. It is very nice of you to devote a whole chapter to my book, and I am much flattered by this, as Sir William Hamilton doubtless was when J.S. Mill wrote an 'examination' of him.

I have now got some offprints of my paper for 'The Aryan Path' — They were sent to me by a mysterious institution called The Indian Institute of Culture, not by the Editor. They are in my rooms in New College, and next time I go there I will send you one.

Best wishes to yourself and your family and thank you again very much
yours sincerely

H.H. Price

p.s I hope you haven't given up on your project of administering mescaline to some of our more common-sensical philosophers. My New College colleagues A. M. Quinton and G.J. Warnock of Magdalen would be good candidates. Both of them have written about perception in an antisense-datum manner.

Letter 13. This concerns a paper I wrote for Nature[42] on the stroboscopic phenomena (the geometrical hallucinations one witnesses on looking at a flickering light) on which I was doing research at Cambridge at the time). It also refers to a talk I gave in Oxford at Professor Price's invitation to the philosophy faculty (or at least some of them).

New College
Oxford
Feb.28th 1957

Dear Smythies,

Thank you very much for lending me this proof, which I ought to have returned before. The chief impression I got from it is the frightful complexity and variability of the phenomena! I cannot quite make out from your description whether these patterns have the property of 'visual depths' (perhaps those described as boiling mud did have it?). So far as I remember the ones I experienced when you tried it on me were perfectly flat. One point which is just new to me is that there can be cortical after-images as well as retinal ones.

I wonder what our common-place philosophers would say about the phenomena. (I think you ought to try the stroboscope on some of them). It seems to me that the language they tell us we must use for describing hallucinations—'I <u>thought</u> I saw..." would not be suitable. But then I don't think it is very suitable for describing hallucinations, either.

It was very nice to see you the other day, and I hope that you were not too much disconcerted by the implacability of Miss Anscombe (I ought to have warned you beforehand that she might be there).

My very best wishes to you all, and especially for the safe and happy arrival of the new baby.

yours sincerely

H.H. Price

Letter 14.

New College
Oxford
September 11th 1958

Dear Smythies,

Thank you very much for your letter. I shall be delighted to see you when you come through Oxford on your journey from London to Gloucester in October. But there are certain days in that month which would be difficult for me. On Friday Oct. 3rd. there is the formal election of our new Warden. On Sunday Oct. 12th. I shall be away all day. On the afternoon of Oct. 16th and Oct. 30th. I shall have Faculty meetings all the afternoon. When term begins (i.e. after Oct. 11th.) I have a class every Wednesday after tea, going on to 7 p.m. But fortunately that leaves a lot of days, and I hope you will be able to come and have a meal with me — lunch, tea or dinner, whichever suits you best.

Shrewsbury, Massachusetts sounds a much more agreeable place than Galesburg, Illinois, and I hope you will enjoy being there. Yes, I have promised to give a lecture at Brown University when I visit the U.S.A. The exact date has not been fixed yet, but it will probably be some time in April or May 1958. I shall not arrive in the U.S.A. until the very end of March. Will you still be at Shrewsbury, Mass. then? If so, I hope you will be able to come over to Brown when I am there. Do you know Professor Ducasse's successor at Brown Professor R. M. Chisholm? I dont suppose that he is interested in Psychical Research at all, but he is a very good philosopher of the "analytic" type, and I enjoyed his book "Perceiving: a Philosophical Study." which I have just been reviewing for the British Journal of the Philosophy of Science.

Best wishes to Mrs. Smythies, to the children, and to yourself.

yours sincerely

H.H. Price

Letter 15.
Hillside
Headington Hill
Jan. 1st 1963

Dear Smythies,

Thank you very much for sending me <u>New Society</u>. I read your article on 'Changing Ideas' with great interest but with some dismay too. It is a gloomy picture that you paint. No doubt a psychiatrist is able to see the seamy side of our present 'Never had it so good' society more clearly than most of us can. I myself am inclined to take a very old-fashioned religious view about it. It seems to me that we suffer from putting second things first and first things nowhere. This is what we Western people have been doing for a long time now, ever since the scientific method was discovered in the 17th century. More and more of us have come to think it obvious that the most important business of mankind is to understand and control our physical environment and the result is the secularistic and technological civilization in which we now live. But it doesn't really profit a man very much to gain the whole world and lose his own soul. This very alarming sentence in the Gospel is now being verified, and we had better try putting first things first before it is too late. The first thing of all is what is called 'seeking for God' in old-fashioned Christian language. 'Seek and ye shall find' 'Knock and it shall be opened to you' are not only recommendations but also empirically-testable predictions. We can try them out for ourselves and see whether they work. It seems to me that they do, at least sometimes. In other words there is such a thing as first-hand religious experience (something very different from holding a lot of logical propositions?). I dont very much mind whether it takes a Theistic form or a Hindu or Buddhist form, so long as it does occur. But I think that human beings cannot be happy, or even wholly sane, unless they have had it in some form or other.

There is however one formidable obstacle which prevents them from even trying to get it, an obstacle which you dont explicitly mention in your paper. You do mention the decline in the belief in an immortal soul. But I think we have gone further than that. We have almost ceased to believe that there is any such thing as an 'inner life' at all, or if we think there is, we have ceased to attach any importance to it. It seems to me that the Behaviourist attack on introspection has had the most [illegible word? 'alarming'] success and has penetrated very deeply into our culture. What is publicly verifiable is what matters. [Thoughts?] are purely private responses and of no interest or importance to anyone, not even the persons who have them. This or something like this is coming to be the prevalent attitude among educated people, and is slowly seeping down into the less educated strata of society. And it cuts religion off at its roots. The seat or locus of religion is the inner life: and all that will be left of religion, if this de-bunking of the inner life continues, will be a sort of Rotarian' get-together-ism', something like what is described in Aldous Huxley's <u>Brave New World</u>. It is not only the immortal soul which has been abolished, but any kind of soul at all, or any kind of not-publicly-verifiable mental life. I remember meeting a very clever young man some years ago who said he did not know what the word 'experience' means.

I apologise for these gloomy reflections which are probably somewhat exaggerated. I dare say that quite a lot of people are beginning to feel that there is something radically wrong with our present secularistic attitude. In a generation or so we—or our successors rather—will probably have quite a different one. But meanwhile we are in a bad way.

Best wishes for the New Year, and thanks again very much for sending me your article.

yours sincerely

H.H. Price

Letters from C.D.Broad to John Smythies.

Letter 1.
Trinity College
Cambridge
Oct. 12th 1955

Dear Dr. Smythies,
Thanks for your letter of October 6th. I have been in Sweden since the end of July, but propose to return to Cambridge tomorrow. Thereafter I shall be very interested to be shown the stroboscopic phenomena which you are investigating.

I heard of you from Aldous Huxley and from Gerald Heard when I was in Los Angeles in the spring of 1954. I thought that Huxley's book on mescal was somewhat irresponsible, but I suppose it cannot do much harm, as it is difficult for the general public to get hold of the drug.

Professor H.H. Price told me of his experiences, when you administered mescaline to him. If it were possible for you to administer it to me, at sometime convenient to both of us, I would be greatly interested. I would, of course, defray any expenses that you might incur.

yours sincerely

C.D.Broad

Letter 2.
Trinity College
Cambridge
Oct. 18th 1955

Dear Dr. Smythies,
Many thanks for your letter of Oct. 14th about mescaline.
(1) I should be very willing for Edward Osborn to cooperate with you in the experiment, if he would care to do so. As he is a busy man, I suggest that you should get in touch with him

and ask him to name two or more alternative dates (preferably week-ends) on which he could come to Cambridge. I should be very glad to put him up in college.

(2) I agree about the advantages of a tape-recorder. If you consult Gauld (who is working at the Psychological Lab.) I think he may be able to put you in touch with a man called Cornall who has one and might be willing to lend it for the occasion.

(3) I have never had jaundice or any other liver complaint. But I am rather easily made sick, &, I should think that dramamine is indicated as a counter agent.

(4) When sober, I am completely indifferent to music & utterly bored with pictures. If you care to use 'a collection of pictures of various artists and a gramophone' to test whether I am otherwise under the influence of mescaline, I have no objection. But I should be surprised if I utter anything but platitudes.

(5) Can you tell me how long one is likely to be before one becomes completely normal again after the sort of dose which you propose to administer. That will enable me to fix a date compatible with my other engagements.

yours sincerely

C.D. Broad

Letter 3.
Trinity College
Cambridge
Jan.29th, 1956

Dear Dr. Smythies,
I have now read the note enclosed in your letter of Jan. 26th. In order to get any further, you ought plainly to consult a mathematician who is familiar with n-dimensional geometry (and, if possible, also with mathematical physics). I grasp the general idea: but could be of little use on technical details, which are surely the essential factor in deciding whether any

experimentally testable results could be anticipated, and, if so, precisely <u>what</u>.

Still, I would like to have a short talk with you soon, in order to clear up some points on which I am doubtful as to your meaning.

I could look into your room at the Psychological Labouratory any afternoon this week at about 2.30 except Saturday. I suggest that you should ring me up and arrange a day convenient to you. I am generally in my rooms from 11 a.m. to 2 p.m. and from 5-7.30 p.m.

yours sincerely

C.D. Broad

Letter 4.
Trinity College
Cambridge
Oct. 31st, 1958

Dear Smythies,

I was sorry to have missed seeing you when you were in Cambridge. I am also sorry to hear of the loss of your brief-case by theft.

I return, as requested, the copy of your paper. I have read it with interest. Bye the bye Hume discusses, and finds no difficulty in the view that some of the constituents of a person's mind, viz visual 'impressions' and 'images' are extended and spatially inter-related. Also Russell should certainly get a large part of the credit or discredit of suggesting that sense-fields are three-dimensional sections of a spatial manifold of a higher dimensionality.

yours sincerely

C.D. Broad

END NOTES

1. Zemach (1986), in a powerful article, dismisses this type of extreme or 'eliminative' materialism as "philosophical science fiction" expressed in an impoverished language (Newspeak) in which one cannot do any science. Edelman (1992) also dismisses it as "silly".

2. My main guides on this journey have been my good friend Arthur Koestler and Viktor Frankl, both of whom dedicated their lives to fight the nihilism of our times.

3. The words Sir George Porter wrote in a letter to the *Times* thirty years ago are as true today as they were then.

"Most of our anxieties, problems and unhappiness today stem from a lack of purpose which was rare a century ago and which can fairly be blamed on the consequences of scientific enquiry. There is one great purpose for man and for us today, and that is to try and discover man's purpose by every means in our power. That is the ultimate relevance of science."

Carl Gustav Jung (1960) says, "The lack of meaning in life is a soul-sickness whose full extent and full import our age has not as yet begun to understand."

In a letter to the *Times* Lord Beloff (1992) wrote to this point:

"It is the dissolution of an individual's sense of belonging to a community, of being part of a network of personal relations, not just a number in the records book of a social security department, that is probably at the root of our discontent...the reason for our ills must be sought in the realm of the intellect."

4. Toynbee, of course, made the mistake, much criticized

by contemporary historians, of thinking that all civilizations, in accordance with Toynbee's Theory *must* decay and collapse. In the past many civilizations have done just that, but this gives us no reason to suppose that ours must do the same.

5.   Alexander Pope.

6.   I am using the word 'culture' here in the anthropological sense.

7.   Lysenko was the Soviet biologist who taught that attributes acquired during the life of an individual can be inherited by the offspring. This is completely false, but appealed to Stalin for propaganda reasons. Stalin made Lysenko the dominant force in Soviet biology for many years.

8.   "Ancient writers were of the opinion that men are wont to get annoted with adversity and fed up with prosperity, both of which passions give rise to the same effects." Machiavelli (1970).

9.   Details of Rousseau's severe personality disorder and paranoia are well documented by Paul Johnson (1988). It will suffice here to quote the opinion of some of Rousseau's contemporaries—Hume's "a monster who saw himself as the only important being in the universe." Diderot's "deceitful, vain as Satan, ungrateful, cruel, hypocritical, and full of malice." Grimm's "odious, monstrous." Voltaire's " a monster of vanity and vileness." Yet people, who had never suffered at his hands and judged him by the quality of his writings, came to a different conclusion "a sensibility of soul of unequalled perfection" (Kant); a "sublime genius" (Shelley—no mean monster himself); "a Christian-like soul for whom only Heaven's Angels are fit company" (Schiller); "our master and brother" (Levy-Strauss). One explanation may be that many of his later admirers based their opinion on Rousseau's *Confessions*, which, as Johnson demonstrates is a tissue of half-truths, outright lies and distortions overflowing

with malice and venom, directed, with much subtlety and disguise, at others. Johnson also traces the path by which Rousseau was led by his own psychopathology to advocate a totalitarian form of government.

10. Rousseau would have particularly disliked contemporary scientific materialism on this account.

11. Herbert Spencer predicted correctly that the bureaucracy in a socialist state will soon develop into an aristocracy and would oppress the workers more ruthlessly than the capitalists ever did.

12. "All our knowledge brings us nearer to our ignorance.
All our ignorance brings us nearer to death,
But nearness to death no nearer to GOD.
Where is the life we have lost in living?
Where is the wisdom we have lost in knowledge?
Where is the knowledge we have lost in information?"

T. S. Eliot from *The Rock*

13. Napoleon was an icon for the Romantics.

14. It is only fair to say that not all philosophers agree with Popper's evaluation of Hegel. But it can hardly be denied that Hegel lent intellectual respectability to the idea of the totalitarian state.

15. Paul Johnson (1988) has also detailed Marx's many defects of character and shortcomings as the scientist he claimed to be. Again Marx's whole philosophy and 'science' derived directly from his own psychopathology. The hatred he laboured to instill into the proletariat to encourage them to rise against their masters was but a pale shadow of the hatred and malice that filled him and that fueled his own apocalyptic vision of man's future. Johnson makes the interesting diagnosis that Marx was really a poet even though he was a (false) prophet at least as evil and unscrupulous as Goebbels. Such inner pain can be projected into the outside world and assuaged

by drowning it in vast plans to change the world by hate. Marx reacted to the miserable condition of the mid-Victorian poor, by doing everything he could to fan the flames of rage, resentment, hatred and thirst for revenge in the hearts and minds of the proletariat. This led eventually to bloody revolution, massacre of many innocents among the guilty, destruction of a fine budding Russian economy, mass starvation, the Gulag and all the horrors of the Stalinist police state, the fires of which have only just burnt out, leaving one sixth of the world in a state of numb misery—for all of which we must hold one miserable little psychopath and his deluded followers, especially the Intelligentsia who should have known better, personally responsible. There seems to be such a thing as contagious psychopathy. It is therefore a fearful indictment of modern Western Academia that many unrepentant Marxists still remain in positions of influence. The Arts and Humanities Citation Index for 1976-1983 lists the 250 most cited authors in these fields. Top of the list comes Marx with 10,788 citations. Second comes Lenin with 6.902! How can civilization survive with these termites gnawing at its very foundations?

17. Reichenbach (1971) says on this matter any clarification of the meaning of 'time' and 'Becoming' can only be answered by science.

18. Germany's leading contemporary composer, Karlheinz Stockhausen, is reported to have gone into a Wagnerian rhapsody at a press conference, in which he described the September 11th attacks as "the greatest work of art in the cosmos...compared to that, we composers are nothing." Presumably he would have regarded the eruption of Vesuvius that wiped out Pompeii as an even greater work of art, to say nothing of Hiroshima. How Hitler would have approved of Herr Stockhausen!

19. Recently the Parek report in Britain stated,

"immigrants owe loyalty to the British state, but not to its values, customs and way of life." This was fiercely attacked (and in my view rightly) by Minette Martin in a leader in the *Guardian* newspaper (May 29th, 2001) on the grounds that culture and race are quite different concepts and only harm results from confusing them. "Multiculturalism" she says "actually promotes racism."

20. Some concrete examples: are the following compatible with Western culture? (i) The ancient Hindu custom of Suttee in which the wife of a prominent man was burnt alive on her husband's funeral pyre and thus gained great honour. (ii) The doctrine that priests should rule, as in Iranian theocracy. (iii) Female circumcision. (iv) The Muslim family custom of killing daughters who engage in premarital sex to preserve the "honor of the family". (v) Infanticide of unwanted females so prevalent in India. (vi) The cruel social ostracism suffered by widows in India. (vii) Animal sacrifice.

21. This passage comes from a review of Bryan Appleyard's savage attack on modern science. Unfortunately the remedy proposed by Appleyard against the ravages of the modern scientific worldview on our psychological health is, believe it or not, the works of Ludwig Wittgenstein!

22. Semmelweiss, it will be recalled, was driven to suicide, for daring to say that the unhygienic practices of the fashionable doctors of Vienna were the cause of childbed fever.

23. Gray (1992) has called for a radical new theory of mind: "What is needed" he says " is, rather, a new theory... that will render the relations between brain events and conscious events "transparent" to use T. Nagel's (New York University) felicitous term. This after all, is the standard set in all other domains of science, so why not here? This new theory is at present unimaginable but only in the sense that no-one could have imagined

relativity or quantum mechanics before *they* were invented, and not because we are dealing with the unknowable or a bad language habit."

Any such new theory will of course be greeted with scorn, ridicule and indifference by the orthodoxy as in the case of Galileo, Pasteur, Semmelweiss, Darwin, Freud, Wegener, and many others.

24. It is also not the view of many budding intellectuals. I recently conducted a survey of my class of 170 senior psychology students at the University of California, San Diego. The first pair of questions were (1) do you think the mind is identical with the brain, and (2) or do you think the mind is something extra that interacts with the brain? A dualist would answer 'no' to (1) and 'yes' to (2): a materialist would reverse these and an epiphenomenalist would answer 'no' to both. The answers showed that 93 of the students were dualists, 53 materialists, 14 epiphenomenalists and only 2 gave incoherent answers.

The next questions asked (3) do you believe that present day science gives a complete account of the universe? Or (4), if not, do you believe that science will ever give a complete account of the universe? To question (3) there were 158 noes and 3 yesses. To question 4 there are 116 noes and 34 yesses.

Question (5) asked "Some religions teach that humans have immortal souls: do you think this doctrine is true?" The result: "Yes'" 84, "No" 57.

Question (6) asked, "Do you believe that the purpose of life on earth is purely biological ("yes" 44) or does it have a spiritual dimension ("yes" 91)? Question (7) asked, "Do you believe that a satisfactory system of ethics can be based purely on current biology and neuroscience ("yes" 28; "no" 103). My last question was "Do you think that consciousness will ever be explained by ordinary neuroscience ("yes" 36); or will this need some new developments in physics ("yes" 30); or will it never be explained by science ("yes" 86)?

Of these students 102 reported a background in the

sciences and 32 in the humanities. This result both surprised and pleased me. It showed that the opinion of the majority of the students was at variance with the nihilistic views expressed by many of the well-known faculty members in this country in the fields of psychology, philosophy and ethics.

25. It is remarkable that Edgar Allen Poe was one of the first to come up with the notion of multiple or parallel universes as van Slooten(1986) has noted.

26. It is also of interest to note, in supergravity theory that postulates eleven real dimensions of space-time, that the extra bosonic field leads to only two kinds of compactification (Freedman & van Nieuwenhuizen, 1985). As they say "In one kind seven of the 11 dimensions curl up into a small hidden structure: such a compactification would explain why the number of dimensions readily observable in the world is four. The alternative is that only four dimensions curl up, and this would lead to a seven-dimensional world." However, it is not at all "readily observable" that the number of dimensions in the real world is four. This only obtains if we identify phenomenal space-time with physical space-time. If, as I have argued in this book and elsewhere, this identification is not legitimate, then, in fact, the uncurled seven-dimensional solution to the extra bosonic field may be the correct one (three dimensions of physical space plus three dimensions of phenomenal space plus one dimension of a unified time dimension equals seven). A similar consideration applies to Kaluza's theory of electromagnetism. In this theory, electromagnetism turns out to be that portion of the gravitational field that extends into an extra fifth dimension of space-time. In order to explain why we cannot see this extra dimension, it is usually stated that we cannot do so because it is curled but so small (diameter 10^{-33} cms) that it is simply too small to detect. However, it is remarkable that no physicist seems to have noticed

that seeing is done by electromagnetism (light rays and electrical reactions in neurons). So the problem is not why we cannot see Kaluza's extra dimension—we see events *with* it! Also events in higher dimensions of space cannot be seen, not because they are curled up too small, but because they lie in what is technically a parallel universe. In exactly the same way an inhabitant of Flatland cannot see events in Cubeland surrounding him, nor can he see events in other Flatlands parallel to his own Flatland that are located in the 3D space, outside his own, that encompasses both.

27.   The difference between Broad's and Price's theories is merely a matter of geometry, unimportant for the ontological and causal aspects of the case. David Lewis (1989) has also suggested that "this world" is just one of many such each spatio-temporally related in this way to ours.

28.   We do not normally move the body-image directly, in spite of the vivid impression the naïve observer gets when he moves his arm. We move the physical arm via activity in the motor cortex generated by efferent mind influences (called psi-kappa). This movement is signaled back to the parietal lobe of the brain by the somatosensory nerves and appears in consciousness (via the afferent brain—>conscious causal system called psi-gamma) as the movement of the body-image that we do experience. People with phantom limbs (that are parts of the body-image) find, however, that they can still move the phantom. This is done by direct connections between the motor and sensory cortices. Most people who are not neurologists, and even many neurologists, do not realize the clinically demonstrated fact that we do not ever experience any events in our own bodies. The somatic events that we do experience are located in the body-image, and not in the physical body that the body-image *represents*.

29.   Ian Stevenson (1997) has presented the empirical

evidence for reincarnation on this planet, based on his own extensive researches in India and elsewhere. Reincarnation may, of course, also be possible on planets in parallel universes.

30. This was written before the death of Diana, Princess of Wales. The reaction of the British people to this tragic event makes it clear that they would overwhelmingly support the sentiments expressed here.

31. Psychiatrists since the days of William James have debated the nature of the religious experiences reported by the Prophet and by St. Paul. It is undeniable that patients with temporal lobe epilepsy report what they describe as very similar encounters with angels or God, cosmic consciousness, feelings of unity with the cosmos, etc.. It is also true that such subjects often develop a keen interest in religious matters and often start writing extensively on the subject. So some authorities have concluded that all religious experiences are due to this illness and are therefore wholly delusional and worthless. However, such experiences also occur in people, who do not exhibit other symptoms of epilepsy and who therefore may not be epileptic at all. Furthermore, it is possible that epileptic disturbances in the temporal lobe may not generate these symptoms *de novo* but may allow contact in some way with deeper levels of reality.

32. Unlike the Bible, the Koran does not have much to say about pure ethics. The longest ethical statement instructs Muslims to be "devout, sincere, patient, humble, charitable and chaste ", to fast and to be ever mindful of God. To those that do this, the Koran promises God will bestow forgiveness and a rich reward. Most of the Koran is devoted to a very detailed and practical day-by-day advice of how to manage one's life, to accounts of the Prophets and of the after-life, of the importance of the Faith, and how to relate to God. This may be partly because

Islam accepts the prophets of the Old Testament as true prophets and so presumably accepts their moral codes. The Koran also says "We [i.e. God] sent Jesus, gave him the gospel and put compassion and mercy in the hearts of his followers." (57.25). Islam reveres Jesus as a prophet but rejects the confused polytheism and doctrine of Redemption injected by theocratic politicians of the later Christian Church.

33.   Most people agree that the Gulf wars were fought to keep the supply of oil in friendly hands.

34.   Unlike Christianity and Islam, Hinduism has no aspiration to become a universal religion and furthermore is no political threat to anyone. Indian culture derives from a great and ancient civilization. Furthermore Hinduism is the most psychologically sophisticated religion in the world. No other religion has a scripture equal in profundity to the Upanishads and Bhagavad Gita.

35.   Erwin Schrödinger was a dualist as the following extracts from his book *Mind and Matter* shows—

"—nowhere, you may be sure, however far physiology advances, will you ever meet the personality, will you ever meet the dire pain, the bewildered worry within the soul, though their reality is to you so certain as though you suffered them yourself—"

"Now our skulls are not empty. But what you find there, in spite of the keen interest it arouses is truly nothing when held against the life and emotions of the soul...If you have to face the body of a deceased friend whom you sorely miss, is it not soothing to realize that this body was never really the seat of his personality but only symbolically 'for practical reference'?"

"Most painful is the absolute silence of all our scientific investigations towards our questions concerning the meaning and scope of the whole display [of the Cosmos]. The more attentively we watch it, the more aimless and foolish it appears to be."

Werner Heisenberg (1959) was also a dualist—

"If we go beyond biology and include psychology in the discussion, then there can scarcely be any doubt but that the concepts of physics, chemistry and evolution together will not be sufficient to describe the facts. On this point the existence of quantum theory has changed our attitude from what was believed in the nineteenth century. During that period some scientists were inclined to think that the psychological phenomena could ultimately be explained on the basis of the physics and chemistry of the brain. From the quantum-theoretical point of view there can be no reason for such an assumption...We would never doubt that the brain acts as a physico-chemical mechanism if treated as such: but for an understanding of psychic phenomena we would start from the fact that the human mind enters as object and subject into the scientific basis of psychology".

36. Smythies J.R. (1953) The mescaline phenomena. *Brit.J. Phil.Sci.* 3, 339.

37. Smythies J.R. (1952) The extension of mind. *J.Soc. Psychical Research*

38. Actually they don't!

39. This led to *The Doors of Perception*.

40. The only other philosophers who took part in these experiments were Broad and Zaehner.

41. Not only public but unobservable: you can't look through the screen of a TV set into its works.

42. *Analysis of Perception.* This was finally completed after I had studied philosophy under Avrum Stroll at the University of British Columbia in 1954-1955.

43. Smythies J.R. (1959-60) The stroboscopic patterns, *Brit.J.Psychology.* 50, 106, 305; 51, 247.

The Moving finger writes; and, having writ,
Moves on: nor all thy Piety nor Wit
Shall lure it back to cancel half a Line
Or all thy Tears wash out a Word of it.

Omar Khayyám